PSYCHE'S KNIFE

PSYCHE'S KNIFE

Archetypal Explorations of Love and Power

ELIZABETH ÉOWYN NELSON

CHIRON PUBLICATIONS

WILMETTE, ILLINOIS

Book and cover design by Marianne Jankowski.
Printed in the United States of America.

Library of Congress Cataloging-in-Publication Data
Nelson, Elizabeth Éowyn.
  Psyche's knife : archetypal explorations of love and power / Elizabeth Éowyn Nelson.
    p. cm.
  Includes bibliographical references and index.
  ISBN 978-1-888602-53-1 (alk. paper)
  1. Love. 2. Interpersonal relations. 3. Power (Social sciences) 4. Sex.
  5. Psyche (Greek deity) 6. Eros (Greek deity) I. Title.

BF575.L8N45 2012
155.3--dc23

2011044022

David Whyte, "No One Told Me," excerpted from *Fire in the Earth*,
© Many Rivers Press, Langley, Washington. Printed with permission
from Many Rivers Press, www.davidwhyte.com.

APULEIUS:THE GOLDEN ASS translated by Walsh (1995) pp.75-77, 84, 89, 91, 102, 111. By permission of Oxford University Press.

FOR BLUE

At least I know this, with sure and certain knowledge:
a man's work is nothing but the slow trek to rediscover,
through the detours of art, those two or three great and
simple images in whose presence heart first opened.

—ALBERT CAMUS

CONTENTS

INTRODUCTION

The soul always reaches deeper than we expect, especially in marriage.
—THOMAS MOORE, *SOUL MATES*

Master storytellers are also master psychologists who know that a person's life is shaped by immense transpersonal powers. The enduring appeal of their work is the juicy engagement between the human and the more-than-human, whether we call it Fate, Destiny, or the gods. This engagement reveals the poignant fragility of life: how much we long for and how little we actually control. "There's a divinity that shapes our ends, rough-hew them how we will," says Hamlet.[1] Plato calls this divinity the *daimon,* the personal companion who accompanies us through life, the one who guides us, and goads us, to remember the story we forgot when we endured the shock of incarnation.[2]

We can glimpse the daimon's influence in part through the stories that haunt us, the ones that, for indecipherable reasons, we must go back to again and again: the novel we reread every year or the film we have watched dozens of times. Such stories may be medicine for the soul: we know we need them but we're not quite sure how they work.

The story that has haunted me is a little embarrassing. I wouldn't have chosen it, frankly. It is a melodrama so well known and so thoroughly studied in my field that one colleague recently suggested it might be an elaborate joke . . . on us. Part of me would be much more satisfied with something obscure and rare, something sexy. But it seems to have chosen me, like it or not. "Eros and Psyche"—sometimes called "Amor and Psyche" or "Cupid and Psyche"—is from a two-thousand-year-old Roman

I

novel. It's a love story between a mortal girl, Psyche, and an immortal god, Eros, so right away we know something: they're going to have relationship problems. Perhaps that's one reason the story has endured. Relationship problems are universal. Another reason is that Psyche is so very human in her complexity and inconsistency. She is tender and ruthless, timid and bold, perceptive and naïve, vulnerable and strong. She acts boldly and regrets her action; she fails to act and feels incompetent; she is confused one moment and clear the next; she exhibits extraordinary faith, then endures deep periods of despair. In other words, Psyche is like most of us. The story, in brief, is as follows.

A king and queen give birth to the third of three daughters, so lovely that the people neglect the real goddess of beauty, Aphrodite, and instead make offerings to the girl, Psyche. She grows up worshipped and alone. Whereas her older sisters marry and leave home, Psyche has no suitors. Perplexed, the parents consult the oracle and are told that their daughter is fated to marry a monster, perhaps even Death itself. They plan a wedding ceremony that will end with abandoning their daughter on a cliff to her terrible fate.

Meanwhile, the years in which Aphrodite has been neglected in favor of Psyche naturally has enraged the goddess. She sends her son, Eros, to aim one of his poisonous arrows at the girl so that she falls in love with a monster. But when Eros flies to the girl—now poised on the cliff, ready for her prophesied marriage to Death—he falls in love with her instead. He whisks Psyche to a secret palace, where he visits her every night to enjoy the ecstatic combats of love. But every day, before dawn, Eros leaves, so that Psyche never sees her mysterious lover.

Months pass, and Psyche's sisters visit. When they hear contradictory stories of her new husband, they grow suspicious. They remind their little sister of the oracle: marriage to a monster, who they believe is merely biding his time before he devours Psyche and the child in her womb.

Now mortally afraid, Psyche confronts Eros with a lamp and knife and discovers that he is a beautiful god. She accidentally pricks her finger on the quiver of arrows and, with that touch of the love potion in her blood, instantly falls in love with her beloved. Eros awakens, outraged at Psyche's disobedience, and abandons her. Psyche, who is heartbroken, longs only for death.

Ultimately, Psyche is persuaded to devote herself to Eros. She propitiates her fearsome mother-in-law Aphrodite and endures four impossible tasks facing her. In each, when Psyche is helpless with fatigue and despair, she receives mysterious help from an uncanny source: ants, a reed, an eagle, a tower. But she fails in the fourth and final task and falls into a deathlike swoon.

The story ends in a conventional "happily ever after" manner: Eros rescues Psyche and publicly declares his love for her. She is transformed into a goddess, and the two lovers, now immortal, celebrate a sacred marriage and soon become parents of an infant girl who they name Pleasure.[3]

Melodrama it may well be, but "Eros and Psyche" also has endured because the name of the central character, Psyche, is the Greek word for soul. We can read the story as an allegory of the soul, specifically the development of the soul in relationship to Eros. Though a simple translation of *eros* is love or desire, it is much more. Eros is what we long for, what we value, and what we create, the force that guides our fascinations and gives substance to our fears. As allegory, "Eros and Psyche" dramatizes a truth that humanity has known at least since the time of Plato: the soul seeks deep and profound relationships. What fascinates me is that issues of power rise quickly to the surface and, in one decisive moment of conflict, the entire story shifts. Yet without the conflict at the center of "Eros and Psyche," we would have no worthwhile story of the soul.

In the end, I love this story for one reason. It has taught me a living truth, as true today as it was two thousand years ago: conflict is evidence that two individuals are engaged in an authentic relationship. Faithful lovers are also worthy adversaries and, when wholeness is called for, beloved enemies.

I

LOST KNIFE

Simple things are always the most difficult.
—C. G. JUNG, *ALCHEMICAL STUDIES*

At dusk, the silence of the lonely rooms grows thick. A young woman walks down the broad stone corridor, caressing the smooth glass of the oil lamp in her hands. The viscous liquid sloshes lazily from side to side as she enters their room. She knows he won't arrive for many hours yet, not until it is dark. It has always been this way. With trembling hands, she sets the lamp behind the luxurious bed and gently touches the cold black wick. Then she turns her attention to the knife.

"You must grasp the two-edged weapon boldly," her sisters had told her, "and with a mighty thrust sever the neck from the head. Only then will you, and the child in your womb, be safe." It couldn't be true, she thinks. She slowly traces the carved hilt with her fingertip but recoils at touching the blade itself. "Remember the oracle," they had said.

The young woman lifts the knife high. As long as her forearm and as wide as her wrist, it possesses surprising grace for something so heavy. In that moment, wondering who to believe or what to believe, she is afraid of her courage and afraid of her fear. She is certain of only one thing: by tomorrow, it will all be different.

As she begins to lower the knife slowly, a last beam of light from the dying day dances along the razor-sharp edge. The young woman realizes it is a living thing, this knife.

Knives aren't terribly ladylike. I suppose that's why they fascinate. For years, whenever I have spoken to another woman about a large, razor-sharp, double-edged knife in the hands of a woman, the response has often been immediate and dramatic: she sits up

5

straight or leans forward, her eyes glitter or she inhales sharply. In a subtle combination of tiny moves—a settling of the shoulders, a lift and rotation of the neck, a rearrangement in the muscles of the jaw, teeth, and lips—she seems to grow more substantial. Her reaction has a distinctive feeling-tone, something creaturely, calling to mind the ready muscularity of a healthy animal. We see it in horses collecting themselves before they leap a fence, in cats who fix their gaze with fearsome stillness, fur rippling with barely contained excitement, and in the alert eye of a great black crow. It is only rarely that this response does not occur, and when it does, there may be a variety of reasons for it. Since I'm frankly fascinated by knives, the women I've spoken with may be responding to my fascination rather than their own. Enthusiasm is contagious. Or perhaps knives per se aren't fascinating, but rather that what captivates is a woman in possession of a volatile, dangerous weapon that really belongs to men. Or so we've been told.

As it turns out, the fascination is not new. Something deep in the human spirit responds to an armed woman, says historian Antonia Fraser. Throughout time and across diverse cultures, armed women have generated "a remarkable outburst of excitement and even awe, sometimes accompanied by admiration and enthusiasm for her cause, beyond the ability of a mere male to arouse" (Fraser 1988, 6–7, 17). The list of armed women in history and fiction is long, from Virgil's warrior Camilla, whose infant clothing was a tiger skin, to the Hindu Durga, the visible incarnation of rage. Other armed women include the widow Judith, who beheaded Holofernes to save the Jews, the Celtic battle goddesses Queen Medb (Maeve) and the Morrígan, and Éowyn, from J. R. R. Tolkien's *The Lord of the Rings,* who plays a decisive role in the battle for Middle-earth. In the last decade or so, the list of armed women includes such pop culture icons Buffy the Vampire Slayer, who's equally handy with a wooden stake, a crossbow, and a quarterstaff, the warrior princess Xena, who swings a heavy two-handed broadsword with ease and grace, Neytiri, the elegant Na'vi warrior armed with bow, arrows, and a dagger in the 2009 film *Avatar,* and Katniss Everdeen, the young heroine of *The Hunger Games,* who is expert with bow and arrow but not bad with a dagger, either.

The armed woman who fascinates me, Psyche, appears in one of our first love stories, where her knife has gone virtually unnoticed for more than two thousand years.[4] The reasons are complex and fascinating, but here is a small taste. When we read "Eros and Psyche" as the story of a young woman in love, perhaps imagining Psyche with her knife disturbs our pleasant fantasies about the absence of conflict in relationships. When we read it as an allegory of the soul, perhaps Psyche with a knife disturbs the quaint notion that the soul is the vulnerable part of us, without a shred of ruthlessness, autonomy, or purpose. This simpleminded view of the feminine soul may help to explain why, over the centuries, readers have more or less willingly accepted Psyche as simple, naïve, and compliant. It seems we have not faced the implications of realizing a more complex, whole, and perhaps troubling understanding of the mythic soul, psyche, which is that the soul obeys its own inexorable drive toward wholeness with or without our conscious consent, and Psyche's knife reminds us of this.

It is time to explore Psyche's knife because it has something important to tell us. To borrow the Chinese aphorism, when the student is ready the teacher will appear. This book proposes Psyche's knife as teacher and contends that some of us are ready to learn.

Love and Power

It is tempting to argue that love and power shouldn't have any relationship at all, except perhaps an inverse one: the more we love, the less power has to do with it. Carl Jung captures the ambivalence we feel about the exercise of power within loving relationships in this provocative statement: "Where love reigns, there is no will to power; and where the will to power is paramount, love is lacking" (1943, par. 78).[5] This is not true. Appealing, perhaps, because then it would be easier to ignore, overlook, or disguise issues of power in love relationships. Or worse, to believe that when we find ourselves engaged in a power struggle with a husband or wife, a child, a sibling, parent, or friend, there's something wrong with us or that love is absent.

Almost nothing reveals character more dramatically than the way we exercise power within love. Then exercising power becomes a skillful art because we are obligated to ask bigger questions that include: What am I creating? and Who am I serving? and How will I live with the consequences of my choices? We don't just slice through an airy nothing, swift, sure, and bloodless. We are more like sculptors working in clay or stone, where each small slice requires us to envision the whole, to hold it in our minds and hearts like a dream, until it slowly emerges. Jung's statement is a romanticized notion of power, in which one must renounce power to become a nobler, loving soul. "So long as the notion of power is itself corrupted by a romantic opposition with love, soul, goodness, and beauty, power will indeed corrupt, as the saying goes. The corruption begins not in power, but in the ignorance about it" (Hillman 1995, 107). We need to examine the opposition between power and love, soul, goodness, and beauty for one reason: power stripped of eros becomes tyranny—the arbitrary or oppressive exercise of authority that is despotic, harsh, severe, and unmerciful. Tyrants show an obsessive need for absolute control in a zero-sum context that selfishly benefits them.

The need for absolute control, the kind of power known as tyranny, historically coincides with patriarchy—the rule of the fathers (*tyranos,* by the way, being the ancient Greek word for "king"). For instance, sociologist Allan Johnson defines patriarchy as "an obsession with control" (2005, 226). This succinct definition should immediately alert us that patriarchy is not exercised exclusively by men and for men. Any woman can be as cruelly patriarchal as a man because, "like their male counterparts," say Marion Woodman and Elinor Dickson, "they live in a patriarchal ethos that operates through control over others, over themselves, over nature" (1997, 4). In fact, the specific image that arises when we think about patriarchy, tyranny, or an obsession with control may be male or female, or androgynous or asexual. It also could be animal, mineral, or vegetable—though I have difficulty imagining a tyrannical sweet potato.

In case any of us is tempted to believe that tyranny is passé, something we have wisely left behind, the popular success of *The 48 Laws of Power*—a well-written and researched homage to Niccolo Machiavelli—should open our eyes. Author Robert Greene simply assumes that *his* worldview is *the* worldview. Power is power over, proving James Hillman's point that the idea of domination dominates our understanding of power.[6] We can hardly escape it, a point I take up at the end of this book. The lesson in Greene's book is that one wins by learning the art of domination in a treacherous, hierarchical world in which the question, Who does this serve? is never asked because the answer is supposedly self-evident: me. "By reading this book you can learn about power in general," he claims, "appearing the paragon of decency while being the consummate manipulator" (1998, xxii).[7] When you are in a situation that does play by these rules, it is good to know it. Then Greene's neo-Machiavellian lessons may be very useful indeed because naïveté is not generally rewarded by tyrants. But it is incorrect to assume that tyranny is the only game in town. We can begin by noticing the obsession with control and by discovering where and how it is present in our lives. Then undertake the more difficult task: give up blaming others—men or males or any one author in the sixteenth century or the twenty-first, for instance—and instead reflect on the ways in which we ourselves are tyrants. Ask yourself, When do I attempt to impose my will on another to serve my own selfish ends? In that moment, you may catch a fleeting glimpse of the tyrant as you imagine him, her, or it. Because any one of us—and any group, organization, corporation, or an entire culture—can become tyrannical and because our entire planet is in dire need of an ethic of care, not control, the urgent question is, How can I find the right uses of power within the context of love? Another way to ask this question is, How can I exercise my power in a loving manner?

Psyche's story teaches us about the artful use of power and the development of feminine potency within the context of what we love and what loves us. I have described the power symbolized by Psyche's knife as *potent,* but not without first considering and discarding other choices. Among these were *virile,* but this has specifically male overtones and doesn't seem fitting to describe Psyche's power. *Vigorous,* which refers to physical or mental strength, energy, or force, was another choice. It also describes the capacity for natural growth and survival in both plants and animals and, when used to describe human behavior, refers to strong feelings, enthusiasm, or intensity. In the end, I chose *potent. Potent* implies an inner mental, psychological, spiritual, or physical strength as well as the ability to exert a strong influence.

9

Seductive lovers and charismatic leaders are potent, though in different ways. An argument can be potent, but so can a drink. Potent also refers to having great self-control and authority. Our potency may exist only as a potential, a power we have yet to realize. This also fits Psyche's story, since "Eros and Psyche" dramatizes the evolution of a soul through repeated conflict and intense suffering. To survive, Psyche must develop her potential and use very precise kinds of power—focus, discernment, perseverance, choice, and sacrifice. The knife symbolizes these.

Learning to use Psyche's knife skillfully has little to do with controlling others. Indeed, an ironical fact about potency is that genuine power consists partly in realizing what one does not control. But it takes a sharp, discerning mind to know this. Naturally, this is where Psyche's knife enters our story.

Psyche's Forgotten Knife

Because "Eros and Psyche" is an allegory about love and the soul—not a theory or concept—it does not offer straightforward definitions that we memorize and shelve in some tidy corner of the mind. Instead the story weaves itself into our feelings and beliefs, taking up residence nearer the heart. As it should. From ancient times to the present, soul always has gone to the core, and it is at the core that we look for soul. Absorbing "Eros and Psyche" as a medley of voices out of our past is like sitting in a darkened theater watching and listening to characters in a play appeal to our emotions and act out our desires. We enter the drama and discover how we, like Psyche, are guided and tortured by what we love, lose, and search for without end. As the story unfolds, we notice which characters fascinate us and which are repellent. If we are very alert, we may even observe what we might otherwise dismiss as irrelevant or uninteresting. What aspects of the myth do we simply neglect?

The question of what we neglect came about when I made a surprising discovery about "Eros and Psyche." There is one piece of the story, one character, who is nearly always ignored: Psyche's knife. How can an object be a character? Through the magic of animation, which was fostered by Walt Disney though it certainly didn't begin with him. In the hands of imaginative animators—who take their cues from imaginative children—brooms fly, teapots speak, and lamps grow bright or dim to express joy or sadness. Just so, Psyche's knife dulls its edge in shame rather than participate in the murder of an inexpressibly beautiful god and it leaps out of Psyche's hand rather than become the tool of her suicide.

Short summaries of the story often describe Psyche approaching her lover holding a lamp, not a lamp *and* a knife. Even scholarly studies of the myth by first-rate psychologists and mythologists dismiss the knife in a few sentences, interpret it in wholly negative terms, or fail to mention it at all.[8] I couldn't quite believe the pervasiveness of the neglect. It was as though Psyche's knife was invisible. In the shock of my initial surprise, I naïvely put a straightforward question to educated people who closely study "Eros and Psyche."

"What do you think about the knife?" I asked.

The response was a blank stare followed by the question, "*What knife?*"

"*What knife?*" I asked, momentarily stunned. "*You don't remember the knife?*"

How could *anyone*, I thought, overlook a shiny, razor-sharp, unsheathed knife in a moment of confrontation between two lovers? Particularly in light of our cultural fascination with fierce women, how could they overlook it when the person wielding the knife is female?

Many people, I found, dismissed Psyche's knife because "it was never used." Yet the blade was sharp, unsheathed, and in play. In fact, those who are experienced in battle know that any naked blade is a threat, which is why unsheathing a weapon signals the beginning of the conflict, no matter what ensues. The moment the weapon slides out of its sheath, with a metallic rasp, a sustained ring, or in stealthy silence, the blade is in play. An unsheathed weapon is a weapon that the combatant is using. If you doubt this, then imagine, for an uncomfortable moment, that you are unarmed and threatened at the point of a knife. Though the knife has not touched your skin, even now the tip wavers slightly in your opponent's trembling hand. Adrenaline floods your body, making you simultaneously flushed with heat and chilled to the bone and heightening your awareness of every nuance of emotion and movement. Remaining completely still, barely drawing breath, you shift your gaze from the naked blade to the eyes of your opponent. She too feels a rush of adrenaline that renders this moment eternal. She too looks surprised, afraid, even confused. But until the edge of that weapon turns away—whether or not it draws blood—she is an armed antagonist who is using a knife.

You may now appreciate Eros's surprise when he found himself facing his heretofore compliant lover holding a lamp and a sharp blade. In no way did he expect Psyche to confront him, not with a lamp, definitely not with a knife; in short, not at all. The assertion "the knife was never used" is simply wrong.

"The knife isn't Psyche's, it belongs to her sisters," is the next reason I heard. This argument is more convincing. It is Psyche's sisters who propose the plan to see and kill the beast. They propose the motive as well. Yet they leave Psyche alone to decide what to do, and it is only after Psyche spends an agonizing day by herself trying to make up her own mind that she resolves on a course of action. Psyche alone prepares the lamp, sharpens the knife, and hides them in the bedchamber. Psyche alone confronts her lover in the dark of night and discovers the god of love.

Forgetting and Remembering

I'm always intrigued by what someone forgets or dismisses. From my experience in working with dreams, I have found that it is often the so-called inconsequential, unimportant, or overlooked element in a dream that releases surprisingly profound meanings, an idea that Freud formalized a hundred years ago in his theory of displacement. What we are inclined to forget is the one thing we need to remember. Jung's theory of the compensatory psyche also emphasizes forgetting. The unconscious, which is revealed in dreams, visions, fantasies, symptoms, oddly meaningful coincidences, and in the deeper strata of myth and story, compensates for the one-sidedness of our conscious attitude. All of these can remind us of other ways of seeing and other things to be seen. As Robert Romanyshyn says so beautifully, "the psychologist is a witness to the unheard stories of an age, what we most desire to forget" (1989, 174).

Why does our age desire to forget Psyche's knife? What about the knife is so repellent that we overlook it rather than look at it?

Interesting question. To explore it, I began to think of "Eros and Psyche" as a collective dream, a text that artists, writers, philosophers, historians, and psychologists have read, analyzed, and rendered in poetry, painting, and sculpture for two millennia. Clearly, it is a dream we have unintentionally misread because we dismiss the apparently inconvenient fact that Psyche confronts Eros with a lamp and a knife. We can easily imagine a trusting and inexperienced girl holding up a lamp to gaze upon her lover. Such a fantasy upholds the conventional view of females, particularly young females, as curious, even interfering, but not prepared and powerful. We recoil when that same girl holds a razor-sharp knife.

Imagining Psyche with her knife reminds us that she is not merely naïve, innocent, and obedient. Like any intriguing protagonist, Psyche makes a choice that irrevocably shapes her destiny. Many scholars fail to mention this at all, treat it in cursory fashion, or view Psyche's decision to confront Eros as a terrible mistake. For example, Bruno Bettelheim argues that Psyche was "tricked into believing Eros was disgusting, with the most tragic consequences" (1982, 11). Marie-Louise von Franz and Erich Neumann think that the true monsters in the story are Psyche's sisters, who sow doubt and suspicion in their little sister's mind.[9] When we agree with these interpretations, Psyche appears as a pawn or a victim, and not a protagonist who makes her own choices. But she does choose, repeatedly, throughout the story. Choosing to confront her beloved is the most terrifying and the most fateful move, a decision she agonizes over for hours and days. The confrontation was sharp, keen, and could have been fatal. It is, without doubt, the pivot point around which Psyche's entire future turns. Readers of the myth do Psyche a disservice by denying her a worthwhile place in her own life story.

There is another shortsighted implication in thinking of Psyche's decision to confront her beloved as a tragic mistake. If only Psyche had not confronted Eros, so this thought goes, she could have continued living a perfect life. In other words, Psyche could have remained the tender, lovely, beautiful girl Eros fell in love with. She wouldn't have felt the shock, shame, and regret at seeing the god and knowing she intended to kill. Nor would Psyche have had to grovel at Aphrodite's feet, endure the terrible wrath of the goddess, and suffer through the four tasks as an abandoned, lovelorn woman. If she had just left well enough alone, none of those awful things would have happened.

The story, however, clearly suggests that leaving well enough alone is not Psyche's destiny, nor is it the soulful choice. Her bold action brings the words of Rainer Maria Rilke to mind: "This is in the end the only kind of courage required of us: the courage to face the strangest, most unusual, most inexplicable experiences that meet us" (Rilke 1993, 88). Psyche has this kind of courage, and we need to remember it.

The Musings of an Armchair Archaeologist

Just as readers of "Eros and Psyche" forget Psyche's knife, it rarely is represented in paintings or sculptures that depict the two lovers. For example, Canova's marble *Amour et Psyche* at the Hermitage Museum in Saint Petersburg emphasizes the tenderness of the lovers, as does another of his marbles, housed in the Louvre. *Cupid and Psyche,* by the nineteenth-century German sculptor Reinhold Begas, is exceptional. It depicts Psyche bending over the reclining form of Eros, before the god has awakened (see Williams 1999, 208). She holds the lamp in her left hand and the knife in her right. However, even in this sculpture, Psyche's knife is not the deadly weapon the text describes. It is small and delicate, scarcely larger than Psyche's hand. In another rare illustration of Psyche with both lamp and knife, the weapon is full-sized but cleverly minimized in another way (see Murray 1935, 191). One has to look very closely at the illustration to see the knife at all, since it is hidden within the folds of Psyche's gown. In the unusual event that Psyche's knife does appear in works of art, it is rendered insignificant.

These artistic renditions of Psyche's knife made me intensely curious about the real thing. The text of the story tells us that the knife is double-edged and razor sharp, which means it would more properly be considered a dagger or sheath knife (Stone 1999, 198). The text is two thousand years old, so what would a dagger from that era have looked like? How heavy would it have been? What materials would it have been made of? And where might Psyche have gotten hold of one easily?

Since I'm not an archaeologist by training, the best way I knew to get these answers is in a museum. So on a trip to London over the Christmas holidays, I found a hotel around the corner from the British Museum and repeatedly visited their collections. (I'm sure they've got my face on security videos somewhere, this strange American woman who avidly studied sharp weapons every day for two weeks, the way someone else might have shopped for shoes or clothes!) I chose to study Bronze Age weapons since this is close to the era in which the tale of "Eros and Psyche" originated.

Among the Late Bronze and Early Iron Age knives, daggers, and swords housed in the British Museum, every weapon identified as a dagger had two sharp edges. Moreover, these weapons are far too large to be easily concealed. Two artifacts tell us why. A Mycenaean bronze dagger (1300–1100 BCE) measured approximately 14 inches from pommel to tip and a central Italian dagger from roughly the same period (1000–800 BCE) measured a full 17 inches. Though this may seem quite large, experts who classify weapons point out that any knife longer than 7 inches but shorter than 22 inches is properly considered a dagger. Greek daggers of the period were typically slight and shaped like stilettos, whereas Roman daggers had thick, V-shaped blades and an average length of approximately 16.6 inches (Thompson 1999, 14, xii). To put this on a human scale, imagine a weapon that extends from the tips of your outstretched fingers to the crook of your elbow with a blade as wide as your wrist.

The only small daggers in the British Museum's collection—similar in size to Psyche's knife as depicted in artwork—were not weapons at all. They were votive artifacts from Sardinia used solely in ritual. If we imagine ourselves in Psyche's situation for a moment, it's easy to see why she would choose a real blade. Warned that she may find a monster in her bed, it's doubtful she would approach the sleeper with a votive object—unless her choice of blade reflects her ambivalence. But this explanation won't do. Votive objects don't need to be sharpened, often can't be sharpened because typically they are fashioned from soft stone or clay, neither of which hold an edge. The story clearly says that Psyche sharpens the blade, a gesture that expresses her serious intent. In the end, I think we must conclude that Psyche is most likely to arm herself with a lethal dagger, which could easily be

16 or 17 inches in length or longer. Such daggers were relatively common household objects in the Roman republic at the time Apuleius wrote the story, something like the handgun in the bedroom drawer of many American homes, though what it's doing in the supposedly perfect palace that Eros provides for Psyche is a very good question indeed.

As we proceed, I invite you to keep this knife in mind: a sizeable, potent weapon, honed until it is razor sharp and ready to kill, a no-nonsense blade for a no-nonsense moment.

From Metal Weapon to Meaningful Symbol

Too often, a living image endures a short, unhappy life, carelessly transformed into a predictable sign long before its full meaning has been explored. Jung speaks about this "monotony of interpretation" when our approach to an image, a dream, or a myth has become "doctrinaire and hence sterile" (1961, 312). Such monotony has been the fate of Psyche's knife and most knives most of the time for one very good reason. Treating them in a more thoughtful, considered way requires time and attention—exactly what people uncomfortable with knives cannot give. The most common prejudice is that knives are always weapons of violence. They maim, wound, and kill.

Even as symbols, knives rarely escape this assumption. For millennia, knives and swords have symbolized the discriminating, rational mind, or logos. This rational capacity includes the ability to differentiate one thing from another, to focus attention, to create logical order out of confusion, and to choose. The principal tool of the discriminating mind is language; logos is often translated as "the word." By association, knives and swords symbolize the discriminating (differentiating) word. As anyone who has been the target of slander or even casual verbal cruelty can attest, words can maim, wound, and destroy with just as much ease as a literal blade. This is especially so when we are vulnerable. A chilling literary example of the destructive power of words occurs in Othello. Iago, arguably Shakespeare's greatest villain, exacts terrible revenge using only words to poison Othello's love and life. This outcome is foreshadowed in Brabantio's ominous couplet early in the play:

But words are words; I never yet did hear
That the wounded heart was pierced through the ear.[10]

Brabantio couldn't be more wrong (in this, as he is in so many things). As the drama escalates, we see just how lethal language can be under the direction of the brilliant and vengeful Iago. Like other knives, Psyche's knife is an image of the human capacity to differentiate, focus, prioritize, and choose. Since this is the soul's knife, however, it partakes of the qualities we associate with soul, which include warmth, depth, mystery, feeling, and attachment. Above all, a knife that belongs to the soul, found and used in the presence of eros, reminds us that knifelike actions affect our shared reality, the intersubjective field where you and I are both separate and not separate, distinct and fundamentally related. "Indeed," says Nathan Schwartz-Salant, "we must move beyond the notion of life as consisting of outer and inner experiences and enter a kind of 'intermediate realm' that our culture has long lost sight of and in which the major portion of transformation occurs" (1998, 5). By focusing on this realm and "allowing it to have its own life, like a 'third thing' in the relationship, something new can occur" (ibid.).[11] When we take up Psyche's knife as Psyche did, we make choices with our vulnerable, emotional bodies and not simply with cool, unfeeling intellect. Such decisions are heart wrenching and gut wrenching. The magnitude of what we may do to ourselves and to others can be overwhelming. Little wonder that our pace in similarly fateful times is slow rather than brisk, that we feel confused long before we are clear, and even clarity is evanescent. Such choices are never black-and-white. We don't walk away clean, quick, and easy. At best we go on, fully realizing what we have chosen to do or not, who to be or not, and who to love or not.

For these reasons, I believe Psyche's knife symbolizes the feeling function, one of the four functions Jung identified in his typological work. Like thinking, the other rational function, feeling requires conscious deliberation. We relate to, rather than repress, our passions and intuitions and emotions, making heartfelt judgments about the bigger questions of life. Like Psyche, we decide what is alive and worth nurturing in our lives and what is dying and must be let go. Many scholars ascribe feeling, relatedness, and receptivity to the feminine, where femininity is a mode of being that is equally available to men and women.[12] The qualities of receptivity, relatedness, and feeling also have been ascribed to the soul.[13] Once again, we see that "Eros and Psyche" can be read in two ways: as the story of a loving young woman—with implications for the feminine in any of us, male or female—and as an allegory of the soul.

The feeling function is so essential that its absence can lead to a grave crisis of identity. The historian Charles Taylor describes this as "an acute form of disorientation, which people often express in terms of not knowing who they are, but which can also be seen as a radical uncertainty of where they stand" (1989, 28). As a result, individuals have no "frame or horizon within which things can take on a stable significance, within which some life possibilities can be seen as good or meaningful, others as bad or trivial" (ibid.). To know who we are and where we stand is akin to using Psyche's knife. Its sharp blade helps us to separate the worthwhile from the trivial, but we must first be willing to take it up.

Those among us who take up Psyche's sharp knife learn skillful discrimination. We are like the gardener who prunes deadwood to preserve the health of the whole plant—only the plant is ourselves and we know that we will bleed a little with each cut of the knife. How do we decide what to preserve, what to discard? According to what values and standards do we make that decision? Even more to the point: according to whose values do we decide? Are our own values really ours or are they hand-me-downs that we have unquestioningly accepted? The myth of Eros and Psyche depicts this task of sorting and separating in rich detail—beginning with Psyche's use of the lamp and knife and continuing through the four tasks imposed by Aphrodite. We can read the entire myth as the development of Psyche's ability to decide, which is an arduous, painful process. Psyche's knife is the symbolic clue to this reading, a forgotten image that, having been silent so long, has much to say.

Trusting the Movements of Our Love

We have only one allegory of the soul, only one story in which Psyche, the soul, is a flesh-and-blood woman with all of the passions and weaknesses that the flesh is heir to. "Eros and Psyche," which dramatizes Psyche's astonishing faithfulness to Eros, teaches us that love and faith are central to the soul's journey. Just as Psyche's fate is entwined with Eros, the soul's fate is always erotic. We work out our fate by discovering what we desire, what we value, and what we would die for.

Psyche without Eros, soul without love, is unimaginable. Just as Psyche is committed to Eros, Psyche's knife is steeped in eros. It is a special blade, a knife so sharp that "it cuts things together, not apart," a memorable phrase from David Whyte's poem entitled "No One Told Me" (1997, 51). In it he writes:

> Speaking and writing poetry
> I unsheathed the sharp edge
> of experience that led me here.
>
> No one told me
> it could not be put away.
> I was told once, only,
> in a whisper,
> "The blade is so sharp—
> It cuts things together
> —not apart."
>
> This is no comfort.
> My future is full of blood
> from being blindfold
> hand outstretched,
> feeling a way along its firm edge.

Once Psyche unsheathed her blade, it could not be put away. There was no turning back after she faced Eros because what was destroyed could not be restored. The lovers could only go toward an unknown future, together or separately or perhaps together and separately. They had no way of knowing what was to come. For this reason, Psyche's knife is an eloquent reminder of the destruction that is a necessary and inevitable aspect of creation. But in the moment, in the immediate aftermath of such a choice, it is simply misery.

The arc of the story shows that Psyche's knife has an edge so sharp that it does cut the lovers together. Yes, they separate physically: Eros abandons Psyche and returns to his mother's house to nurse his wounds. She wanders, alone and forlorn, tempted by the serenity of death. Yet within their individual solitude the lovers are more spiritually bound than ever before. The legacy of their story, considered as an allegory of the soul's journey, is the enduring connection between love and soul.

Readers of "Eros and Psyche" can observe Psyche's drive to become a unique, whole individual—though Psyche herself, like most other characters in myth, shows scant self-awareness. Jung named this drive individuation, and he believed that it was the most universal form of human creativity (1921, pars. 757–762). If we create nothing else during our sojourn on earth, each of us will feel the urge to create ourselves. When we do, we must decide between two paths: remaining a *puer aeternus*, a perpetual child who is "all promises and no fulfillment" (Edinger 1992, 14) or becoming a substantial individual, unique and irreplaceable. The *puer* can "do anything but he can't decide on one thing in particular. . . . In order to make a real accomplishment he must sacrifice a number of other potentialities. He must give up his identification with original unconscious wholeness and voluntarily accept being a real fragment instead of an unreal whole" (ibid.).[14] The substantial individual commits to a course of action, endures the chaos of feelings this choice brings about, and also endures the unforeseeable consequences the choice sets in motion. James Hillman describes individuation as recognizing the daimon, who motivates, protects, invents, and "persists with stubborn fidelity" and who "often forces deviance and oddity upon its keeper, especially when it is neglected or opposed" (1996, 39). Above all, the daimon "cannot abide innocence" (ibid.). Some part of us may want to escape reality and remain naïve and childlike but another part of us insists that we face life in all its sublime and fearful complexity.

Psyche's life is marked by deviance and oddity from the start. Aphrodite and Eros are the twin archetypal powers that shape her destiny, and Psyche matures in relationship to them. Thus "Eros and Psyche" dramatizes a truth that humanity has known at least since the time of Plato: the soul needs relationships of the deepest and most profound kind—which includes periods of intense conflict and struggle—because intimacy with another illuminates the self. It is a sacred *agon*, the Greek word for struggle and the root of our noun *agony*. The Psyche who approaches the bedside, in the depths of night, armed with lamp and knife, teaches us that faithful lovers are also worthy adversaries. Anything less simply will not do.

Across the centuries, "Eros and Psyche" speaks to all of us who believe life without profound love is worthless and that love without conflict is impossible. Sylvia Perera, writing about the myth of Inanna, expresses the emotional core of "Eros and Psyche": "The intimate one opens the deepest wounds, and lovers, thus, become enemies. And they are also beloved enemies, since the woundings create separations across which fresh passions leap" (1981, 80). Conflict is evidence that two individuals are engaged in an authentic relationship. Confrontation creates the possibility of a fresh encounter and a stronger union.

ALCHEMICAL KNIFE

*Individuation therefore also means separation, differentiation, the
recognition of what is yours and what is not. The rest has to be left alone.*
—MARIE-LOUISE VON FRANZ, *ALCHEMY*

*As she remembers her sisters' advice, Psyche shudders at their
vehemence. "You are living in the foul intimacy of a furtive love,"
they had said, "and your husband—or so you call him, though when,
indeed, was your wedding ceremony?—your own husband prohibits
you from seeing him lest his true form be revealed." Their eyes had
glittered with strange intensity. "He is a monster who will devour both
you and your child. We know this. We are certain of it. You must kill
him to protect yourself."*

*Just before they left, Psyche's sisters had vowed to remain steadfast
allies, instantly available to carry away the treasure once her loathsome
lover was dead. Then they would arrange a truly enviable marriage
for Psyche, human being to human being. And the monsters would be
banished once and for all.*

*With this, the sisters had departed, leaving Psyche alone and even
more miserable, with only the echo of their dire warnings and a clever
plan to kill her lover. Could she do it? Would she do it? Psyche would
soon know this and so many other things now that dusk dimmed the
quiet corridors of the empty palace and Earth herself seemed poised in
suspense.*

Jung had great respect for our limited ability to fathom the
deep psyche and its abundance of archetypal figures, objects, set-
tings, and themes. "Not for a moment dare we succumb to the illusion that an archetype can be finally explained and disposed of,"

he said. "The most we can do is *dream the myth onwards* and give it a modern dress" (1951, par. 271). Our myths are thousands of years old, and we live them anew every day. But do we recognize them in their modern dress?

Taking a fresh look at a familiar story, "Eros and Psyche," from the archetypal perspective of Psyche's knife, and giving it the attention it well deserves means "seeing through" the knife, an activity James Hillman calls psychologizing.[15] We begin by exploring the deeper symbolic meanings suggested by the thing itself, and then we endeavor to see through those meanings, too, always maintaining a sense of wonder and possibility. This method is one familiar to artists and poets, anthropologists and archaeologists, mythologists, and psychologists, who trust the native eloquence of the image and render the insights it offers as faithfully as possible in paint, clay, melody, choreography, or text.[16] We'll follow Jung's lead and use the language of alchemy to see that Psyche's own story is an alchemical opus, a sacred work.[17] This is especially apt for "Eros and Psyche" because the annals of alchemy produce a fascinating precursor to Psyche's knife: the principle of creation called the Logos-cutter. The Logos-cutter symbolizes the unity of the cosmos that was created through a process of separation. In language eerily reminiscent of David Whyte's poem "No One Told Me" (cited on p. 19), the separation of the cosmos doesn't simply cut things apart. It "also cuts things together. In every case the division was not only a separation but a reunion, for the Logos was the Glue as well as the Cutter; that is, it was the principle of cohesion which makes the universe a unit in spite of its manifold divisions" (Edinger 1985, 189).

As we read "Eros and Psyche," we see that Psyche's knife is just such an alchemical blade. We become alert to a particular stage of alchemy, *separatio* (separation), that runs like a steady bass beat throughout the myth, and to how separation serves union. As odd as this may seem, in this story it's inevitable: Psyche's knife is the soul's blade and the soul conjures eros. By the end, Psyche's knife teaches us the full emotional complexity of the phrase "beloved enemies." Eros and Psyche are allies and they are foes; they love each other and they wound each other; they act with sweetness and with suspicion; they are adoring and contemptuous, beguiling and manipulative, faithful and bitter. All of the contradictory emotions and impulses are important to the story—as they are essential to any whole relationship—and, taken together, they shape the journey of the soul within the context of eros. In fact, Psyche's knife has an edge so sharp that it cuts these contradictions together rather than cutting them out or away. Differentiation intensifies relationship.

In western Greece there once lived a king and queen who had three daughters. The eldest two were beautiful but the youngest, Psyche, was so incomparably lovely that no words could describe her. Never before had the people of this kingdom seen her like, and they began to view her as a fresh incarnation of the goddess of love herself, Aphrodite—only this new Aphrodite was truly a virgin, untouched and pristine. As word of her loveliness spread far and wide, travelers flocked to the kingdom to worship Psyche as the new goddess. In their eagerness, the people neglected the altars of Aphrodite.

When the true Aphrodite realized that the honors due to her were being granted to a mortal, she was outraged and vowed revenge. Aphrodite sent for her winged son Eros, told him the entire story, and showed Eros the miserable girl who had usurped the goddess's place. Aphrodite begged Eros to let fly one of his arrows and make Psyche fall in love with a vile and disgusting creature. Then she kissed him long and hungrily and left.

Time passed, and Psyche's older sisters eventually married noble husbands. But though Psyche grew more beautiful with each succeeding year, no man dared approach her. She was worshipped by all—and she remained untouched and alone. The king her father, concerned that the gods were angry, consulted the oracle. To his horror he was told to dress Psyche in funeral robes to meet her spouse, for she was fated to marry a monstrous, terrifying bridegroom. On the designated day, the king and queen and all the people mournfully conducted Psyche to a high cliff, chained her to the rocks, and left the young woman to face her destiny.

Psyche waited and trembled, then felt the gentle breath of the West Wind. It grew stronger and stronger until it lifted her up and carried her down to a lush, green valley. When she awoke, she saw a forest with a fountain in the center and a magnificent palace that only divine craftsmen could have fashioned. Drawn by its beauty, Psyche timidly walked inside and found that the rooms were filled with radiant, golden light. Then a voice welcomed her, saying, "All that you see here about you is yours. We shall attend to your every need." Psyche looked for the speaker but saw no one. Then a different voice offered Psyche a refreshing bath, while still another invited the young woman to a banquet fit for a queen.

As dusk descended and the palace grew quiet, Psyche retreated to the bedroom. When it was full night, she heard the sound of approaching footsteps and trembled in fear for her virginity. Moments later, someone entered the room, joined Psyche in bed, and tenderly made love to her. Before dawn her unknown lover left. Psyche never saw who he was.

Psyche's life continued in this new and mysterious way. By day, a devoted staff of invisible servants attended to her every need. By night, Psyche and her unknown lover enjoyed each other's tender embrace. Though it was lonely, she grew accustomed to it.

Psyche's Childhood

"Eros and Psyche" opens in territory familiar to readers of myths and fairy tales. Psyche is the third and most beautiful daughter of a king and queen. Unlike her sisters, she is not destined for a normal human life. She isn't even regarded as wholly human. Because of Psyche's extraordinary loveliness, she is treated as a fresh incarnation of the goddess of beauty herself, Aphrodite. The crowds drawn to Psyche are "dumbstruck with admiration at her peerless beauty" and "revere her with devoted worship" (Walsh 1994, 75). If you're human, being revered and worshipped demands a heavy price, as many celebrities will attest. Psyche knows this. She has Aphrodite's beauty but not her joy. Perceived as a goddess, Psyche is quite literally untouchable, which condemns the young girl to a lonely existence. "All admired her godlike appearance, but the admiration was such as is accorded to an exquisitely carved statue" (77).

The cruelty of Psyche's fate becomes even more apparent as she comes of age and grows into her full beauty. Just as she was admired from afar by strangers as a child, she is now admired from afar by suitors. No man who might have wanted to marry Psyche dared approach. How does one propose to a goddess? Thus from the very beginning of the story, the most significant detail about Psyche's life is that she is isolated and alone.

Psyche's early experience of isolation culminates in a desolate fate. When no man seeks her hand in marriage, the oracle at Delphi explains why. Psyche is destined for marriage with death. How does she respond? Not as we might expect from a supposedly naïve and tender girl. The prophecy doesn't surprise her. Psyche is the only one who knows that her grief began when everyone saw her as an incarnation of Aphrodite (Neumann 1956, 69). With preternatural wisdom, Psyche intuits that she has been the living corpse that her community prepares for the marriage for a long time. Psyche is so alienated from her family and her community that there is ominous resignation in her question, "Why should I postpone or shrink from the arrival of the person born for the destruction of the whole world?" (Walsh 1994, 76). We also hear Psyche's inability to discriminate her future from the future of the world. It's all one overwhelming catastrophe, which is why, in cognitive psychology, this is known as catastrophic thinking. She does not understand death as a necessary part of life, nor can she distinguish between literal death and symbolic death—the many endings that are part of a larger cycle of death and rebirth in any vital life.

The first part of "Eros and Psyche" ends with the death marriage. Family and community abandon Psyche in a ritual act of sacrifice that forever divides her life. Standing alone on a rocky promontory, she awaits the arrival of her monstrous husband with a terribly human mixture of insight and ignorance. Readers of the story do not know yet what is to come, just as Psyche doesn't. We only know what the oracle foretold, marriage, which combines separation and union in a single transformative ritual.[18] We separate from family and childhood, surrendering one life, and unite with the beloved in creating a new life. At the deepest level, all genuine marriage is a symbolic death and rebirth. What this feels like day by day is unique to each partnership.[19]

Psyche in the Palace of Eros

In the next part of the story we follow the course of Psyche's so-called married life in another splendid palace. This new dwelling, although opulent and beautiful, is scarcely less isolating than Psyche's childhood home. Instead of being worshipped like a statue, she is treated like a princess. For someone hungry for ordinary human relationship there is little difference between them. By day, invisible servants feed, bathe, clothe, and entertain her. Delectable food is placed before her, brought not by human hands but unsupported on a gust of wind, and a singer enters and performs unseen. By night, an "unknown bridegroom" enters her bed. She did not choose him and is never permitted to see him. Understandably, Psyche is terrified. She trembles and shudders in fear for her virginity and dreads the unknown presence more than any other menace.

One interesting detail emerges from closely reading this part of the story. When the west wind carries Psyche from the cliff, it lays her down outside the palace. Psyche chooses to enter. I wonder if she was seeking refuge. I wonder if any of us, needing refuge and sighting a beautiful palace, would stop to wonder what we're about to enter and how it will change us.

Once inside, Psyche discovers a very odd place: a setting that offers every comfort without the most ordinary comfort of all, companionship. Just as Psyche once accepted her community's adulation as a new Aphrodite and the ritual marriage to death, she accommodates herself to her so-called marriage. She is characteristically passive and appears to enjoy it. Since she is waited on hand and foot, perhaps there is genuinely little to complain about except loneliness, which Eros's nightly visits partly assuage. As the god of love, we expect him to be a skillful lover. And it's true that Eros loves Psyche enough to secretly defy his mother, Aphrodite. But is it a perfect life or is it a luxurious prison? An even better question is how is it both?

As we go forward, bear in mind that there may be perfection in wholeness, but there is never wholeness in perfection. The Self— the archetype of wholeness who silently and invisibly conducts the individuation process in each of us—will disturb, cajole, and importune in any number of remarkable ways, particularly when everything appears perfect.

One night, Eros warned Psyche that her sisters had just heard of Psyche's fate and were looking for her. A visit with these sisters, he warned, would bring great sorrow, even disaster, and he forbade Psyche to welcome them. At first Psyche complied with his command, but her loneliness was overwhelming. She pleaded with her new husband to allow just one visit with her sisters, using words and gestures so endearing and seductive that he finally relented.

Psyche's sisters made their way to the rocky cliff where Psyche had been abandoned and wept loudly. The West Wind carried the sisters down to the palace, and the three young women were joyfully reunited. Psyche offered her sisters all the luxuries of the palace, which they viewed with astonishment and envy. What kind of man could afford all of this? And so they asked Psyche to describe her husband, but of course she could not. Psyche had never seen Eros. For it was Eros, Aphrodite's son, who had sequestered Psyche in a lover's paradise, against his mother's wishes and far from the prying eyes of all the world. To disguise her ignorance, Psyche described her new husband as a young and handsome hunter with a downy beard. She immediately sensed her sisters' disbelief and grew afraid. Psyche heaped gems and jewels in her sisters' laps then hurried the two out the door.

The sisters were suspicious and furious that their little sister had so far exceeded them in wealth and fortune. They complained bitterly of their own lot and began to scheme how to bring about Psyche's destruction.

Eros, meanwhile, warned Psyche what her dangerous sisters were up to. "They will urge you to see my face," he warned her, "but this you cannot do. You must not answer any questions about me at all." Then he told her a piece of wondrous news. "In your womb, a child is growing. If you keep our secret, the child will be born a god. If not, it will be mortal."

Again and again, in the strongest language, Eros warned Psyche of her sisters' malice, wickedness, and hatred until finally Psyche burst into tears and promised never to try to see the face of her beloved. Now that she was pregnant, Psyche would soon see Eros's visage in the face of their child, and that was enough for the new mother. "Only grant my wish to see my sisters once more, and I will be content." Eros, once again enchanted by Psyche's words and kisses, relented.

The sisters clearly endanger the pristine existence Eros has created for himself and his lover. They are malicious and hateful and driven by envy. Envy, one of the seven deadly sins in the Christian tradition, is defined as blindness of the heart in the Book of Common Prayer. Thomas Moore, using different language, says much the same thing: envy is "an inability to see what is closest to us," which he describes as hyperopia of the soul (1994b, 114). When our hearts and souls are blighted by envy, we lose touch with the potential value of our own fate and have elaborate fantasies of others being blessed with good fortune. As we shall see, Psyche's sisters are eager to take Psyche's place, not because they are capable of a truly erotic or soulful relationship, but because the splendid palace is the proper setting for a life of glamour, prestige, and power. Like Psyche, the sisters fail to see how the palace of Eros is also a prison.

Before the second visit the sisters hatch a plan of revenge. They greet Psyche with false smiles, feign joy at the upcoming birth, and ask again about this mysterious husband. Psyche lacks their cunning and forgets what she had already told them. So she invents a different description of Eros. Armed with this proof of Psyche's duplicity or ignorance, the sisters grow bold, unequivocal, and imperative. They tell Psyche, who is now pregnant, that the oracle was correct. She is undoubtedly married to a monster who creeps around the palace oozing deadly poison. "You're being fattened for slaughter," they tell Psyche, "and your unborn child is simply richer fare for the patient beast, who intends to devour you both" (Walsh 1994, 89). They finally coerce Psyche into admitting her ignorance. She tells them her husband has threatened her with great disaster when she shows curiosity about his features. No matter how much she longs to see him, he forbids it. Psyche implores the sisters to help her without suspecting an ulterior motive.

Psyche's inability to fathom her sisters' motivation is the most telling evidence of her naïveté. Yet it also demonstrates the cost of deprivation. Denied all human contact except the two visits with her curious and maleficent sisters, Psyche gratefully accepts whatever crumbs of attention she gets. Her isolation makes her hungry for ordinary human connection regardless of the danger. It also diminishes her ability to evaluate potential danger. Psyche has long hours by herself but no one to help her reflect on her situation. She cannot discriminate the kindness of her sisters from their cruelty. She also cannot discriminate the fact—the oracle foretold Psyche's marriage to a monster—from conclusions the sisters draw about that fact, which may or may not be true. Psyche has never seen her husband, but does that make him the prophesied monster? Yes and no.

On the one hand, Psyche's sisters never do see Eros, either literally or metaphorically. They have no understanding of eros, the need to connect, feel, or love; they are consumed by envy.[20] Psyche is the envied little sister, an object of their anger more than a human being. On the other hand, the sisters' envy is a form of sight. In their small-minded attempt to spoil Psyche's life, they paradoxically expose the rottenness at its core. They see through the display of wealth and luxury to the actual monstrosity in the relationship, though they themselves don't know it. Whereas Eros is not literally a monster, Psyche is seduced and held captive in a monstrous sham marriage with a lover who expects compliance and refuses to be seen or known. True, the sisters can be accused of impiety toward a god. But without their actions, Psyche may have continued to piously worship a husband who enjoyed marriage to a suppliant, not an equal. The sisters' envy ultimately deepens Psyche's insight into her relationship to Eros. It also hastens its end.

Just so, unwelcome "ugly" emotions or thoughts often bear the seed of truth. For instance, when we hear something repugnant and feel ourselves recoil defensively—"that isn't true!"—we might take a moment to pause and reconsider. Could it be true, no matter how hateful or ugly it is? Is it more likely to be true because I don't like it? Such questions aren't easy to answer, but they can alert us to the shadowy aspects of any situation: what we don't want to see, feel, or admit. It takes skillful, feeling discrimination to examine our feelings. It takes Psyche's knife.

Psyche Confronts Eros

Psyche is clearly uncomfortable with her intention to confront Eros with a lamp and a knife, but there is nothing in the story to suggest that she is uncomfortable with knives. Nor does it suggest that her sisters are uncomfortable with knives or ignorant of their use in a fight. In fact, the advice they give Psyche shows a fair degree of expertise. The sisters tell her how to sharpen the knife and where to hide the weapon so that she can quickly and quietly retrieve it in the darkness, and then they tell her how to use it. "Grasp the two-edged weapon boldly," they advise, "and then with all the force you can muster sever the knot which joins the neck and head of that venomous serpent" (Walsh 1994, 91). Then they leave Psyche to do the actual deed.

And she does. As the long tumultuous day draws to a close, Psyche finds a lamp and a knife and prepares for the confrontation in solitude. This turn of events raises an intriguing question: How is it that Psyche so easily gets hold of a knife? It isn't difficult to imagine Psyche finding a lamp, a standard household object even in a palace. We could also imagine her retrieving a knife from the kitchen—had she even ventured into that part of the palace. But the text is very specific, and Psyche's knife is no cooking tool. It is a razor-sharp, double-edged dagger. We cannot definitively say that it is hers, but we also cannot say that it isn't.

Though Psyche is afraid and uncertain, she does carry out the first part of her sisters' plan that very night. She grasps the lamp in her left hand, the knife in her right hand, and approaches the bed.

That night, after Eros lay fast asleep, satiated from lovemaking, Psyche stealthily crept out of bed to retrieve the lamp and knife. As she approached the sleeper, the light revealed an astonishing sight. Her unknown husband was none other than Eros, the beautiful god of love. At this breathtaking sight, the lamp brightened with joy and the knife dulled its edge in shame. Psyche, suddenly aware of her deadly intention, tried to hide the knife by plunging it into her own breast. But the knife, refusing to commit suicide, slipped out of Psyche's hand and dropped to the floor at her feet.

Psyche continued to gaze upon the enchanting beauty of Eros. When her eye caught the brace of weapons near the bed, she curiously began to examine them. She held up an arrow, tipped with the poison that heats the blood of Eros's victims. But because she was still trembling at the discovery of the god, she accidentally pricked a finger on one of the sharp points—and passionately fell in love with the god of love. Psyche drank in his extraordinary beauty with even more passion and began to kiss him fervently. Just then, a drop of hot oil leapt from the lamp onto his shoulder and painfully scalded his unblemished skin. Eros awakened, saw Psyche, the lamp, and the knife, and flew out of bed in a rage.

Psyche piteously clung to Eros as he flew above her head, but to no
avail. He ignored her tears and pleas and scolded her in bitter words.
"Poor, simple Psyche. Look what you have done! I warned you what
would happen if you disobeyed me and now you and your sisters will
suffer the consequences."
And with that, Eros left.

Psyche's desire to see and know Eros is our first glimpse of the
bold and aggressive soul. It also reveals her longing to be seen
and known more fully. This is a critical point: she does not gather
her shaky courage to destroy a relationship. She wants to transform it through seeking deeper intimacy in which both she and
her beloved are more fully known to each other. What Psyche
does not understand is that her action is already transformative:
she has broken the rule Eros decreed, subtly altering the balance
of power.

When the lamp illuminates the sleeping figure of Eros, Psyche's
gaze is insatiable and penetrating, taking in every detail of her
lover's appearance: his golden head and luxuriant hair steeped in
ambrosia, his neatly pinned ringlets that stray over his milk-white
neck and rosy cheeks, his dewy wings that gleam white with flashing brilliance. Psyche intuits correctly that the goddess of beauty
herself would be glad to claim this glorious creature as her own
son. Psyche's hunger to see Eros is sharp, yet for all the aggression in her gaze, lingering over Eros's beauty requires holding the
beloved in her attention. That's why we often say that we "behold"
something that evokes awe or reverence, something numinous.
It captures our imagination and, as we hold it, we are simultaneously held. These experiences are ecstatic, literally outside of
movement and outside of time. They have been described as soul
moments or flashpoints of eternity (Cousineau 1994, xx). Such
was Psyche's first sight of Eros.

At this point in the story, we become distinctly aware that the
lamp and knife are not merely passive tools in the hands of active
human beings. They are fully autonomous, dramatis personae in
their own right. Upon seeing Eros, the light of the lamp burned
more brightly and the knife dulled its edge in shame. Then, as
Psyche realizes she had intended to kill this supposed monster,
she turns the knife on herself. But the knife prevents this death,

too, and falls out of her hands. This is an important point, which becomes clearer by comparing this story with similar moments in two of Shakespeare's great tragedies. Imagine, for instance, that the knife Juliet used to kill herself in *Romeo and Juliet* had refused to commit murder, dulling its edge in shame. Or imagine that Othello's strong hands, acting according to their own will and conscience and repulsed by the idea of strangling an innocent, suddenly grew weak in the moment Othello wrapped them around the neck of the sleeping Desdemona? The independent action of the knife is crucial to the overall plot of "Eros and Psyche."

After the knife drops out of Psyche's hand, the young girl, still in shock, trembling and confused, finds herself irresistibly drawn to Eros's weapons—the quiver of arrows that the god of love uses to penetrate others. She tests one of the points with a trembling hand and accidentally wounds herself, infusing her blood with the love potion. She falls in love, and Eros awakens. Literally, the god wakes up and symbolically Psyche's own eros, her erotic connection to the beloved, is awakened.

In a sappy film, this might be the moment the lush romantic music swells, the lovers look into each others' eyes, and the audience renews its faith in happily ever after. Not so here. Eros is shocked that his compliant girl-bride has disobeyed; his vanity is wounded. He flies into a rage, hovering above Psyche while she clings to him, unhappy and in dread of his leaving, already regretting her actions. And then, exhausted, she falls—unable to hold onto or follow her beloved.

Eros places himself above Psyche literally and metaphorically to add just the right note of contempt to his anger. At this moment, he appears to hold all of the power and she none of it. In fact, there is something terribly poignant in the image of Psyche clutching Eros as he ascends and then falling to the earth in exhaustion. It makes her vulnerable mortality and his arrogant divinity apparent. Also, it is at this moment that Psyche (and the reader) begin to see that she must live with the consequences of her actions, a painful fate for any of us.

In light of the story as a whole, we can see that the relationship Psyche destroyed needed to end. But Psyche, a suffering human without the godlike ability of foresight, does not have even the omniscient vantage or the emotional distance of those who watch the drama unfold. She is a mere human being, as we all are in such moments, overwhelmed with feelings of loss and regret. Psyche does not consciously know whether or not her decision to act was a good one, though even she, given the opportunity to reflect, might admit that some part of her knew it was. In such a moment, however, few people can readily distinguish what is rotten from what is still good and bravely consent to let go when it is time. Like Psyche, we often cling to the last vestiges of what is dying or dead, and often it is only exhaustion that compels us to release our hold.

Psyche's knife preserves the lives of the lovers, and it also preserves their love. Although Eros abandons Psyche, not once does he say he no longer loves her. In fact, the vehemence of his anger at the moment the lovers see each other face to face dramatizes Eros's fiery passion and not his cool indifference. The erotic connection between them appears as strong as ever. Moreover, the ending of the story suggests that Eros, still spiritually bound to Psyche, undergoes his own healing transformation. After a period of time spent cloistered in his mother's house, perhaps nursing his burned shoulder and singed pride, he seeks out Psyche when she needs his help. Eventually, Eros is willing to defy his powerful mother openly, in front of the assembled Olympians, which I'll discuss more below. Life, love, and the ability to endure enormous suffering prevail, even to the point of restructuring relationships between the human and the divine.

Regret and the Sharp Edge of Experience

The one person who sustains the dynamic, connecting quality of eros uniting the players in this dramatic field is Psyche. She alone remains troubled, uncertain, and vulnerable to the events taking place. For this she is accused of being simple, weak, and child-like—which says a great deal about those who judge Psyche and perhaps less about Psyche. Another way to describe Psyche is that she is receptive or open to as many aspects of the conflict as she can tolerate, including the irresolvable conflicts within herself. Whereas the sisters and Eros sustain their tough implacability and arrogance, Psyche is tender. The other equally tender characters are, oddly enough, the lamp and the knife. Psyche, lamp, and knife embody the complex and paradoxical emotional aspects of the conflict, including determination and ambivalence, fear and love, delight and horror, awe and shame. It is particularly ironic that Psyche's knife, a lethal weapon, ensures that Eros and the erotic relationship between Eros and Psyche do not die.

The young woman who confronts Eros is naïve rather than wise. Psyche feels everything, but she cannot discriminate among her feelings or effectively act upon them. The ability to discriminate would help her gain distance and create more interior space in which to rearrange and place events, looking at them from many different angles (Hillman 1975, 30–31). For instance, Psyche knows quite a bit about Eros when her sisters begin interrogating her. But she doesn't evaluate it carefully and completely, weighing her sisters' words against the evidence of her senses. Instead of sifting through her impressions, she is easily caught up in a single point of view. Psyche needs the particular power that the knife symbolizes, the ability to separate the confused heap of facts and feelings she faces, the ability to sever her own judgments from those of her sisters. She also needs it to distance herself from them so that she can cut through the illusion of their loving concern to the malevolent envy that it barely disguises. At this point in the story, she can do none of these things.

Psyche is not alone in her naïveté. As it turns out, Eros was naïve to think that Psyche would be compliant. He is caught unawares, and his contemptuous reaction to his surprisingly bold lover betrays fear as much as it expresses anger. I suspect that this is because Eros, though physically a man, is emotionally immature, a son who has yet to leave his powerful mother. He is not yet the powerful phallic god that he will eventually become. For instance, though he aggressively takes what he wants in rescuing Psyche from the rocky cliff, he does not have the wherewithal to declare openly that she is the woman he loves. Their so-called marriage remains clandestine for Eros's benefit. On the other hand, the fact that he ventures into any kind of intimacy at all with Psyche suggests something deeply important stirring within.

Eros's wounds are a burned shoulder and singed pride. As a metaphor, these wounds are particularly apt. Burns are immobilizing because the body's immediate response is to form a thick crust of scar tissue to protect the vulnerable flesh underneath. Nonetheless, a full recovery requires the injured person to move and stretch to prevent permanent immobility. It is excruciatingly painful, slow work, and since the healing process begins from the inside out, there is scant evidence that any change is taking place at all. Eros's situation is truly pitiable. And from another perspective, the wound that Eros suffers from is being stuck in his problem. He has been symbolically grounded, which is not a happy circumstance for a god with wings.[21]

In the hands of a mature soul, Psyche's knife could be a fine tool. It could symbolically grant individuals the alchemical wisdom to see that cutting things together, not apart, is evidence of a truly sharp edge. At this point in the story, Psyche cannot hold the knife in either way—as crude killing weapon or as fine tool—and so the knife itself exits the stage, never to appear as such again. However, one way to view the remainder of the myth is as a sequence of lessons in the use of the alchemical knife. Over the course of an intense initiation journey, Psyche develops from naïveté to wisdom by honing her power of discrimination. Psyche's tasks challenge her to separate, extract, and choose from a deeply embodied place of feeling rather than a cool or distant intellectual stance. She never picks up a literal knife again, but she takes up the knife as a metaphor over and over as she learns to become a discriminating, individuated soul.

Despair and Revenge

Psyche believed that all was lost. She left the palace and threw herself into the river, but the river, fearful of offending Eros, bore her up and carried her to the opposite bank. There Psyche encountered the god Pan teaching his beloved Echo how to play the pipes. When he saw the forlorn girl, he immediately knew that she was suffering the pangs of love. "Do not try to kill yourself," he advised, "but go instead to the god of love and plead with him. Though he is a spoiled and wanton youth, surely he will relent."

Psyche left, but she wandered aimlessly. After a time, she found herself in the kingdom where one of her sisters ruled, and so she sought an audience with her. "I did as you advised," Psyche told her, "and discovered that my husband was none other than the god of love. He

abandoned me with bitter words and said he knew that he had married
the wrong sister. Now he means to make you his bride."
Psyche's sister was overjoyed by this news. She ran to her husband,
inventing some excuse for her sudden departure, and then quickly
made her way to the rocky promontory where the West Wind had twice
carried her safely to Psyche's former home. The sister leaped into the
air, eager for the arms of Eros, and fell to her death on the crags and
boulders below.
Psyche wandered on and came to the kingdom of her other sister,
whereupon Psyche related the same story. This sister, likewise eager to
trade a despised mortal husband for the god Eros, met the same violent
fate.

After Eros abandons her, Psyche's despair is so intense that
she again tries to commit suicide. Who wouldn't understand this?
The young woman is steeped in loss, death, abandonment, and
mourning. She has lost her home, family, and community, she has
endured a ritual marriage to death, she has witnessed the death of
her relationship with Eros, and she has discovered that her sisters
envy and despise her. She is an exile, a truly solitary wanderer
for the first time in the story. As Psyche is about to throw herself
into the river to drown, the god Pan tenderly intervenes and tells
the grieving woman to direct her prayers toward Eros—the very
same god who has abandoned her. When I imagine this moment,
I'm in awe that Psyche would even consider Pan's suggestion,
no matter how wise or well-meaning. Seek out the person who
has abandoned one? Volunteer for more cruelty, humiliation, and
rejection? These questions prompt us to consider who and what
Eros truly is, perhaps for the first time in the story. It is as though
the loss of Eros the beloved widens our sensibility to eros, as we'll
see when we follow Psyche's journey.

Psyche faces a stark choice: life or death. She chooses to live,
letting her sorrow and despair become an ordeal of faith. Psyche's
longing for Eros becomes a font of fresh passion that fuels the
search for her beloved.

Psyche's first important gesture after listening to Pan should
compel us to question our assumptions about the tender soul.
This is another moment in the story where her ruthlessness is on
display, however satisfying the outcome may be. She visits first

one sister, then the other, using just the right words to beguile them with an empty promise that appeals to their vanity. "Eros married the wrong sister," she tells each one. And barely have the words left her mouth when they rush to the cliff, the place of Psyche's marriage ritual, and vault into empty space. Psyche is not exactly a murderer, but by taking advantage of her sisters' corrosive envy she is certainly complicit in their deaths. Once again, we see a supposedly naïve and tender young woman capable of ruthless behavior.

The deaths of the sisters bring to mind one of Jung's more chilling statements: "The unconscious has a thousand ways of snuffing out a meaningless existence with surprising swiftness . . . even when death consists only in the cessation of spiritual progress" (1955–56, par. 675). I interpret Jung's statement to mean that there are many kinds of death. And the walking dead—those who maintain only a semblance of life—are truly horrifying.

Meanwhile, Aphrodite received word that her disobedient son had retreated to her home, where he nursed his painful wound. She was outraged that he had failed to do her bidding and had fallen in love instead of making Psyche the miserable bride of some monster. She let it be known that she was looking for the young woman to exact revenge.

Psyche continued to wander over the land, looking for Eros. She chanced upon a temple and stayed to tend it with respect and care, not knowing which of the gods she served or whether she might gain news of her beloved. When Demeter appeared, Psyche asked for the goddess's protection. Demeter, fearful of antagonizing Aphrodite, refused. Psyche wandered on and found yet another temple, this one dedicated to Hera. Again Psyche begged for protection, and again it was refused.

Psyche understood the meaning of these refusals and decided to waste no more time. She would seek out her mother-in-law, the great Aphrodite, to beg her forgiveness and appeal for mercy. Psyche made her way to Aphrodite's home, not realizing that as she approached her most dangerous enemy she was also drawing closer to her beloved Eros.

When Psyche appeared at the gates of Aphrodite's temple, the servants gleefully dragged the young woman inside to face the full wrath of the goddess. "So you finally decided to pay a visit to your mother-in-law," the goddess asked in a furious voice. "Well, if it is pity for yourself and my future grandchild you expected, think again!" With that, Aphrodite attacked Psyche, tearing her clothes, her hair, and striking her again and again. "Where is your beauty now, you worthless girl? Do you have any strength, or value, or perseverance left? We shall test your mettle and see!"

With these ominous words, Aphrodite locked the young woman in a room and assigned her the first of four impossible tasks.

Psyche's next important gesture occurs before her encounter with Aphrodite and the often-analyzed trial of four impossible tasks. As Psyche searches for Eros, she accidentally discovers first one, and then another temple in disarray and spends time restoring them to order. Although she does not know who she is serving, her actions demonstrate an instinct for the sacred, the respectful attitude needed to serve the divine in all its forms. Psyche's challenge at this point in the story is to seek a particular deity, because although all powers must be served, not all powers are alike. Psyche intuits this. She asks for sanctuary from Demeter and from Hera, and when they turn her down for fear of angering Aphrodite, Psyche does not ask why. She realizes that she must face Aphrodite herself, and she talks herself into this decision by saying, "Why don't you surrender yourself voluntarily to your mistress, and soften her savage onslaught by showing a humble demeanor, however late in the day?" (Walsh 1994, 102). And so she goes to her most implacable enemy, symbolically placing love's wound at love's altar.

Facing the Terrible Mother

From the beginning of the tale, Psyche's fate is shaped by the fact that she arouses the envy of Aphrodite. The goddess is wholly justified in her anger. She, the ancient mother of the universe, has been neglected. "The Gods want to be remembered . . . and they do not ask forgiveness for their havoc, so that their havoc is also remembered" (Hillman 1975, 188). Aphrodite is even angrier that her devotees begin worshipping a mere mortal in her place because it belittles Aphrodite, the one crime she abhorred above all others. A story in the Homeric hymns, for instance, tells of a vengeful Zeus who once arranged for Aphrodite to become helplessly and miserably infatuated with a mortal, Anchises, specifically to embarrass the goddess. After spending a wondrously erotic night with him, Aphrodite's farewell to Anchises is the bitter recognition that "there will be great disgrace for me among the immortal gods every single day continuously because of you" (Boer 1970, 81).

In addition to losing her devotees to Psyche, Aphrodite also suffers a blow to her vanity from much closer quarters. Her treasured son Eros, the one whom Aphrodite kisses "long and hungrily with parted lips," not only disobeys her but becomes "miserably, unmentionably" infatuated with Psyche (Walsh 1994, 77). It is no wonder that she assumes the terrible aspect of the goddess. When Psyche finally meets Aphrodite face-to-face for the first time, the goddess abuses her physically and verbally. "Oh, so you have finally condescended to greet your mother-in-law, have you? . . . You can rest assured that I shall welcome you as a good mother-in-law should" (104). Aphrodite then summons her two maids, Melancholy and Sorrow, and orders them to torture Psyche.

Psyche makes no attempt to defend herself. She wisely surrenders to Aphrodite and, in service to the goddess, probably comes to know her more intimately than others whose lives are less entwined with archetypal love, beauty, and desire. The quality that most characterizes Psyche during her service to Aphrodite is patient endurance. Psyche is the last person who imagines herself capable or prepared, yet she perseveres. Psyche's incapacity to adopt a tough, self-sufficient, heroic stance makes her an alluring figure. She is not a winner, but she does prevail, and all of Aphrodite's furious attempts to belittle Psyche ultimately amount to nothing. In fact, they have the opposite effect: Psyche is ennobled by enduring the goddess's wrath.

The four tasks Aphrodite assigns to Psyche, though they are quite different, exemplify the alchemical process of *separatio* (separation) or a variant of it called *extractio*. She completes the first three with helpers—an army of ants, a river reed, and a soaring eagle—who arrive at an opportune moment and take pity on the sorrowful Psyche. Each is in preparation for the final task, a harrowing journey into the underworld that Psyche must complete alone.

Inside the locked room, Psyche faced the first of four impossible tasks. In the center of the floor was an enormous heap of mixed seeds, barley, millet, and other grains, which Aphrodite commanded the girl to sort by nightfall. Psyche could not imagine how it might be done. She sat down, bewildered and forlorn, not noticing her first helpers. An ant, followed by thousands more, crawled toward the seeds. With patience and determination they sorted the entire heap into many separate small mounds. When Aphrodite returned at dusk she was shocked and suspicious. "Well I know that this is not the work of your own hands. But so be it, I will give you another task."

The next morning, Aphrodite commanded the young girl to go out into the wilderness where a particularly beautiful herd of sheep grazed. They were the ferocious rams of the sun, prized for their brilliant golden fleece. "Collect some of the fleece for me, girl," Aphrodite said, expecting the rams to kill Psyche. Once again, Psyche could not imagine how it might be done. In despair, she wandered down to the river, once again contemplating suicide. She was so numb that she barely heard the words of wisdom offered by a green reed: "Psyche, do not approach the rams directly. Instead, lie down in the shade and rest awhile. Later, when the sun begins to set, go to the meadow where the rams have grazed and collect the bits of fleece caught on the low-hanging branches. Offer this to your harsh mistress. When Aphrodite saw that the worthless girl had completed the second task, her eyes narrowed suspiciously once again. "I know this is not your wisdom or skill. But, I will give you another task."

Aphrodite handed Psyche a delicate crystal flask. "Take this and fetch me water from the river Styx." Psyche was aghast. She knew that its waters were poisonous even to the gods. With dread, she walked toward the place where the fierce waters tumbled over a sheer cliff into a deep gorge below, unable to imagine how she would fulfill this third task. At that moment, Zeus's eagle took pity on Psyche, swooped down and grasped the flask in his talons. Skimming gracefully next to the deadly water, the eagle filled it and returned the flask to the girl. When Psyche delivered the flask to Aphrodite, the goddess was even more enraged. The next task, she knew, would be the girl's last.

Psyche's first task, exemplifying *separatio*, is to sort a heap of mixed seeds into separate piles by morning. At the moment she is most desperate, help arrives in the form of tiny ants, creatures known for their discipline and patience, who take pity on Psyche and busily sort the seeds for her. Their timely help suggests that when the soul feels overwhelmed and confused, discipline and patience are needed to create order out of the chaos. Psyche's second task, exemplifying *extractio*, is to gather golden fleece from the rams of the sun, fierce and dangerous animals likely to kill anyone who wanders too near. A green reed whispers that there is another way: instead of approaching the rams directly, in broad daylight, Psyche should wait until the evening when the rams have passed through a grove. There, some of their fleece will catch on the low-hanging branches and Psyche can safely extract the fleece from these. She learns to gather just the amount she needs, indirectly but effectively, perhaps suggesting that small moves suit the soul. Psyche's third task is also a lesson in *extractio*. Aphrodite commands her to fill a flask from the fast-flowing Styx, a river whose waters are deadly even to the gods. As before, Psyche cannot use a direct approach, but once again she doesn't need to. The royal bird of Zeus, the eagle, flies to her assistance. Its ability to soar above the landscape before advancing in a swift and precise way dramatizes the wisdom of broadly viewing an entire situation before choosing the most effective approach.

In reflecting upon the first three impossible tasks through the prism of the alchemical knife, Psyche learns how to use its power in a subtle and thoughtful way. Psyche's knife is a fine tool for sorting, separating, and extracting rather than a destructive weapon that maims or kills. Just so, when facing chaotic or overwhelming situations in life we can use our own symbolic knife to make fine, feeling distinctions and prudent, soulful judgments. This is an artful exercise of power that affirms the value of relationship instead of ignoring, denying, or abusing them; an expression of the soul's devotion to eros in service to archetypal love and beauty.

Psyche's fourth and final task was beyond compare: she was to go down into the underworld and collect a beauty ointment from Queen Persephone. Psyche was well aware that no mortal ever returned from such a journey; few gods could safely navigate this realm. In despair,

Psyche spied a tall tower and again planned to kill herself. But the tower took pity on her and offered this advice: enter the underworld prepared with two coins for the ferryman and two honey cakes for Cerberus, the three-headed dog who guards the gates. "All along the journey," the tower warned, "there will be lures to keep you from your purpose. You must resist each one. Above all, do not open the ointment from Persephone, for it will be deadly to you."

And indeed, when Psyche entered the underworld, the lures were cleverly arranged to tempt the kind-hearted girl. A man whose bundle of wood had tumbled from the back of his donkey asked her to stop and help him; Psyche refused. Crossing the river Styx, a corpse floated to the surface of the water, one cold hand lifted in a plea for help; Psyche refused. Queen Persephone, who readily granted the request for a sample of her beauty ointment, kindly invited the exhausted girl to feast before returning to Aphrodite; Psyche refused. Weary yet determined, Psyche made her way back to the opening between the worlds.

Then Psyche paused. She considered the jar of ointment and lifted a hand to caress her own careworn face. "Why should I simply give this to Aphrodite?" she wondered. "Why not use some of it myself, to recover my beauty so that my beloved Eros will be irresistibly drawn to me?" With that, Psyche opened the jar—and immediately fell into a Stygian sleep.

At that moment, Eros felt something stir. He had languished in Aphrodite's palace long enough; now it was time to leave. As he flew toward his beloved, Eros discovered that the wound to his shoulder had healed. He scanned the landscape and, spying the sleeping Psyche, Eros kissed her awake and promised to make all things well. He flew to Mount Olympus and petitioned the father of the gods, Zeus, for the lawful right to marry Psyche. Zeus, who loved Eros, granted his wish. To appease Aphrodite and keep the peace, Psyche was welcomed among the Olympians as the newest goddess. Shortly thereafter, the assembled gods were delighted with another addition to their company when Eros and Psyche gave birth to their child Pleasure.

Psyche's fourth task is more complex and difficult. Like the second and third tasks, it is a lesson in *extractio*, since Aphrodite requirement of Psyche is to collect a small amount of ointment from Persephone. Psyche must hold her goal firmly in mind, turning away from anyone or anything that might tempt her to hesitate, turn back, or wander. And she must know when, where, and to whom to give the precious resources she brings with her: two coins and two honey cakes. At any moment, a faltering commitment means death. The fourth task is an extension of the training Psyche has received from the first three: she must not only discriminate one thing from another, she must know that in the act of discriminating, some things are ignored, others are appeased, and still others are left behind. To select one path is not to select others.

The meaning of Psyche's last task and the events leading into the ending of the story are hotly debated. Some find the narrative satisfying, some don't. I personally find the conclusion of the last task unbearably sad. When Psyche does reflect for a moment on her travails, she is primarily concerned with their effect on her appearance. She doesn't notice how she has demonstrated love, courage, faithfulness, endurance, or any number of other exemplary qualities that constitute the enduring beauty of character or nobility of soul. She is afraid she has grown physically ugly. Psyche believes the ointment she retrieved from the underworld is the remedy; only then, she thinks, will I "be pleasing to my beautiful lover" (Walsh 1994, 111). Psyche cannot distinguish between internal beauty and external beauty, nor can she distinguish between what belongs to humanity and what belongs to the gods. Psyche also cannot distinguish among the kinds of beauty conferred by each deity: Aphrodite's beauty is different from that of Artemis, which is different still from the beauty of Apollo, Hera, Hecate, or Dionysus. Persephone's beauty is of the underworld, infused with death. Among her many names, she is known as the Queen of Destruction. But Psyche fails to anticipate the effects of a deathly cosmetic. As a result, she falls into a deathlike sleep when she opens the box. Thus Psyche survives the journey to the underworld but not the return.

From the myth of Eros and Psyche, we do not know whether Psyche ever learns the difference between internal and external beauty or whether she learns any other lessons. Her swoon sets into motion a train of events in which Psyche is removed from the human world, deified on Mount Olympus, and lawfully wed to

Eros in an eternal union. This is, ironically, the final act of *extractio* in the myth. Psyche is plucked from Earth and assumed into the Greek pantheon. We are left with a divine soul but no flesh-and-blood body to teach us about the ongoing encounter between ourselves and what we love.[22]

Awakening Eros

It is important to make a distinction between what we learn while reading "Eros and Psyche" and what Eros and Psyche learn while living the story. Is the only story that we have about the soul truly a story of Psyche's transformation? Or is it merely a story of her deification? There is no clear answer. True, the tasks Psyche faces, beginning with her confrontation of Eros, grow increasingly difficult and complex. Partly for this reason, we can view the story from a developmental perspective. Yet Psyche shows no awareness of any development. Like other mythic characters, she is not self-reflective, nor does she see herself at the center of her own story. Psyche's inability to complete the final task suggests that she learns nothing at all. The plot is resolved through an act of god; indeed, through the acts of two gods, Eros and Zeus. When we read the myth literally, Psyche appears to be a bit of a ninny, a typical helpless female who collapses at the least whiff of a challenge. Taken literally, it seems like just another story that follows the tedious plot of boy meets girl, boy loses girl, boy rescues girl, throwing in a few equally tedious stereotypes such as the vindictive, jealous sisters and evil mother-in-law. Aren't we done with all that?

This is where a symbolic reading of the myth, and an alchemical reading of the knife, is so suggestive. For instance, Psyche's fate is marriage to death. Eros's actions fulfill Psyche's fate in a profound and paradoxical way. In their palace, she is dead to the world she once knew, dead to the world of ordinary reality, and as Eros's compliant and accommodating partner, dead as an individual. Psyche exists in the liminal state of the initiate undergoing a profound transformation. She is betwixt and between two worlds or two lives, in service to the goddess Aphrodite who assigns her four tasks of increasing difficulty, a number that has been symbolic of wholeness, eternity, and the soul since the time of the early Greeks (Mahdi, Foster, and Little 1987, 5).[23]

Although Psyche must complete the four tasks without human help, supernatural assistance is consistently available to her. Might this mean that the soul is never bereft and alone, but always embedded in something larger? The ants, the reed, the eagle, and the tower are the quiet voices that come to Psyche's aid. Perhaps they would have come to anyone, but there is little doubt that the depths of Psyche's despair—the great existential quiet in which she repeatedly contemplates suicide—prepared her to listen for them and to them. Perhaps Psyche's story demonstrates something Jung said: truth does not speak with a loud voice, great quiet is needed to hear it.[24] In that quiet, perhaps we are more apt to feel our way into the thick atmosphere of the *anima mundi,* the ensouled world, where the tendrils of every form of matter interweave in a great glistening web. Awareness of the living matrix of matter is an ancient idea, emerging in many esoteric traditions, including alchemy, and reappearing today in quantum physics. It is an especially fruitful way to consider the relationship between Psyche and Eros because "alchemical thinking offers an appreciation of the depth and mystery of relationship which can allow one to experience a space that is animated, that is alive with meaning, and that contains its own process" (Schwartz-Salant 1998, x).

Psyche's fateful journey takes her into realms she never dreamed of, which is what most of us say about similar moments in our own lives. As many have discovered, it is the return from the underworld, exactly where Psyche fails, that is the most difficult part of the journey. In some respects, the piece of her story we most need to guide our own journey is the one we don't have. Yet Psyche's failure to deliver Persephone's ointment to Aphrodite—the beauty treatment of the gods, not meant for humans—does teach us something crucially important. One of our life tasks is to recognize in a heartfelt and soulful way what we most value, feel, and cherish, what is ours and what is not. The rest has to be left alone (von Franz 1992, 256). Psyche's knife, truly an alchemical blade that cuts things together, helps us to understand this. To borrow Edinger's lovely phrases again, it compels us to become "a real fragment" through the commitments we make in work and in love instead of remaining "an unreal whole," committed to nothing (1992, 14). Living this tension between real fragment

46

and unreal whole is the fine art any of us can practice with the one material we have available, our embodied human life. Psyche's journey dramatizes this art and serves as an evocative reminder that soul-making is fundamentally creative. Or as Jung puts it, "We must not forget that only a very few people are artists in life; that the art of life is the most distinguished and rarest of all the arts. Who ever succeeded in draining the whole cup with grace?" (1933, 118).

Readers of the story, mere mortals, are left to wrestle with the meaning of every aspect of Psyche's journey, not just this last poignant failure and the deus ex machina of the ending. But I suspect that the dissatisfaction so many of us feel with the ending is, ironically, a compelling invitation into the story. It is a stark reminder that our own soul journeys are never complete and never without failure, yet we don't quit the journey or hide from the gods. We may be tempted, as Psyche was, but like her we also find the help we need to be indefatigable and unerring in our devotion to eros. In that place, we meet Psyche with soul.

Another Version of the Story

At the risk of insulting Psyche's knife, who has taught me so much, I have fantasized a different version of the tale. In this version, Psyche never needs the lamp and the knife to confront a monstrous relationship because the alchemical knife—our power to differentiate one thing from another using our deepest feelings in the most honorable way—plays a vital role earlier in the story. Does this mean that Psyche will not meet other monsters on her journey or avoid facing other harrowing choices? No. But in my fantasy, the community, especially its leaders, teach Psyche that we are not gods and goddesses and that the limitations inherent in being human are also part of its grandeur.

In western Greece there once lived a king and queen who had three daughters. The eldest two were beautiful but the youngest, Psyche, was so incomparably lovely that no words could describe her. Never before had the people of this kingdom seen her like, and they began to view her as a fresh incarnation of the goddess of love herself, Aphrodite—only this new Aphrodite was truly a virgin, untouched and pristine. As word of her loveliness spread far and wide, travelers flocked to the kingdom to worship Psyche as the new goddess.

In their eagerness, the people of the kingdom neglected the altars of Aphrodite. But Psyche's parents foresaw the danger and protected their daughter from this unwanted attention. When people began to leave fresh flowers and delicacies outside the palace gates as offerings to the young girl, the king and queen intervened. They spoke to the people, telling them to honor the gift of beauty in everything, not just in one human girl, no matter how lovely she may be. And they planned a great ritual procession to Aphrodite's altar, leading the people to express their gratitude in a reverent spirit.

As their daughter Psyche grew lovelier with each passing day, she too understood that love and beauty are precious gifts, not to be taken lightly, and honored the goddess in her many forms. Eventually the young woman began to lead the community in tending the altar of the golden Aphrodite, and everyone gave thanks to she who infuses all of earthly life with such loveliness.

One day, the form Beauty assumed was a lovely and loving man, who saw more than Psyche's physical allure. He cherished her soul.

On the eve of the young couple's wedding, the queen presented her daughter with a small, beautifully wrapped box. Psyche, ever curious, opened it to find an intricate gold and ruby broach shaped like a branch of flowering pomegranate. "It is right and just that we honor Aphrodite," the queen said, "but we must never forget Persephone, Hades's bride, who rules the underworld."

As the queen pinned the golden broach to Psyche's robe, the daughter noticed a shadow flit across her face. "Why Persephone, mother? She seems to make you sad."

"Not sad, no. Pensive, perhaps. Wiser, I should hope," the queen said, as a small smile played around her mouth. "A visitation from Persephone reminds me of the true complexity of enduring love: the choices we must make, the separations we must endure, the reunions that bring us joy." She paused. "But this is not something I can teach you, sweetheart. Only she can."

Meeting Eros with Soul

In the end, it is clear that "the true story about Psyche is the one that involves Eros, that the soul realizes itself in relationship, that human love is directed toward soul-making" (Downing 1988, 43). The terrible, painful irony is that Psyche's commitment to Eros deepens once the lovers separate. From that point on, she knows Eros not as a nightly presence but as an irreplaceable absence. Psyche's despair at the thought of losing him forever drives her to repeated attempts at suicide. For Psyche, life is worth nothing without Eros. Yet Psyche herself does not fully understand who or what the absent Eros is. In the misery of mourning, who among us can think clearly? Our entire being traumatized by loss, we repeatedly try to understand what happened, what is happening, what will happen. If and when we are ready to go on without the one we love, we can perhaps begin to see and feel what part the beloved played. Where is the hole, the emptiness, the place that is frozen or rotting or dead? Which piece was he or she? How many different pieces?

In our story, Eros becomes both absent guide and guiding perspective, affecting everything that Psyche is and yearns for. The lovers are divided in one way, but remain inextricable. Let's remember, though, that such a grand psycho-spiritual view, no matter how true, eludes Psyche. She is a flesh-and-blood woman, agonizing over the loss of the beloved. Nonetheless, her very persistence for the sake of what she loves redefines the heroic: "She can stand up to the disintegrating power of the archetypes and confront them on an equal footing. Yet all this does not occur in a Promethean-masculine opposition to the divine, but in a divine, erotic seizure of love" (Neumann 1956, 143). On her journey, Psyche discovers what John Keats calls "the holiness of the Heart's affections and the truth of the Imagination" (Cook 1990, 365). Her imagination, to borrow the poet's language, seized the astonishing beauty of Eros as truth, her truth. In that moment, she discovered her beloved in a new way.

Here I am compelled to return to a core theme. None of this would have happened had Psyche remained timid and compliant. Instead, by confronting Eros with lamp and knife and destroying an envied relationship that appeared perfect, Psyche set in motion every other key development in the story. She courageously engaged her fate and faithfully served the gods who shaped her life, no matter how fearsome, cruel, or terrible. Our own fate may make a similar demand. In that moment, will we have Psyche's courage to sacrifice a so-called perfect relationship to become whole, no matter what agony this engenders? Will we be able to take up Psyche's lamp and knife not knowing how it will all turn out—whether we're making the right choice or the biggest mistake of our lives? Her story is a marvelous and chilling example of rare courage. It has a happy ending. Ours may not.

How do we know what choice to make? There is no easy answer, but "Eros and Psyche" offers a slender clue that has to do with place. The story unfolds in a sequence of distinct locations, each of which is the dramatic setting for one part of Psyche's journey. These include Psyche's childhood home, the palace of Eros, and finally the wide world where Psyche performs the first three tasks and the underworld, where she journeys for the fourth task. The final location is Mount Olympus, where the sacred marriage to Eros is celebrated before an audience of the gods. Except for this last, where the tale ends, Psyche must leave each place or die. Leave or die—that is the choice. If we think of each of these places as a psychological moment as well as a physical location, Psyche's journey requires a series of symbolic leave-takings, an old-fashioned word that suggests both letting some things go (leaving) and carrying some things with her (taking). Doing this intentionally requires careful sorting, an embodied differentiation symbolized by Psyche's alchemical knife.

Most of us know by our late teens or early twenties what it is like to leave our childhood home. In fact, we probably recall with greater precision the time leading up to leaving. Emotions often include tension, frustration, resentment, and anger—which, if they are intolerable, may devolve into apathy, depression, and listlessness. We may dream of walls closing in or shuttered windows or clothing that's too tight or becoming lame. Developmental psychologists, particularly those studying perinatal experience, say that this late adolescent experience recapitulates the trauma of birth, the womb being first home we must leave. So whether we are about to emerge into the world as infants or as adults, the choice is stark: leave or die. Psyche's story alerts us to the fact that this stark choice can occur anytime we have outgrown a place and that what feels like death may also be birth.

Leaving one's birth family to enter adulthood is a common rite of passage in Western culture. Leaving the home we share with our beloved—the choice Psyche must make—can cause far more anguish because it is in such sharp contrast to that durable fantasy "until death us do part." How do we know if a relationship is dead and that leaving is the right move? The tale of Eros and Psyche gives us a hint: full, clear, and complete knowledge is unlikely, if not impossible. Psyche did not intend to leave or to be left. She only knew that something was wrong and risked everything to look closer, to see her beloved and be seen by him. She was following eros, seeking a deeper and more profound relationship to her beloved. Ironically, she awakened eros in more ways than she anticipated.

Let us imagine eros as that creative, connecting force continually giving birth to the soul, continually drawing us onward toward greater participation in life. It's risky, confusing, and frightening. It takes the kind of courage Psyche demonstrates, which is not showy or uplifting or heroic in any conventional sense. She conquers nothing except perhaps her fatigue and despair—and I'm not even sure she conquers that. She lives it every moment of every day, as though it were a spiritual practice.

Like Psyche, we may have no vision of where eros will lead, but that cannot stop us. Follow we must.

3

SACRIFICIAL KNIFE

Only that which can destroy itself is truly alive.
—C. G. JUNG, *PSYCHOLOGY AND ALCHEMY*

As the knife clatters to the stone floor of their bedroom, ashamed of its murderous intention, the lamp flares with joy at the sight of the gorgeous god. Too late it realizes that eagerness, too, can offend, when a drop of hot oil spills onto the gleaming skin and awakens Eros.

Eros feels his shoulder burn most painfully, then notices the unnatural brightness of the bedroom and the shocked gaze of Psyche. Eros is stunned that this poor, simple girl would dare disobey him, a god! Well, she would soon learn the cost of this transgression, he thinks.

Without uttering a word, he darts away. Still, Psyche manages to cling desperately to his right foot. As he feels her hands weaken, her grip slip away, and watches as she slumps to the floor, Eros hovers high above in triumph. Never before had the distance between god and mortal been so apparent; he feels disgusted at himself for ever having loved her.

"My mother warned me of you," Eros says bitterly, "but too late I see that she was right, that I should never have degraded myself—I, the most beautiful of gods, the son of a great and powerful goddess—by taking you as my wife." His voice is full of contempt and rage. "But not even she, my immortal mother, ever imagined that you would disobey me. Very soon you will learn, Psyche, what you have lost and what you have gained: a lifetime of regret and misery."

And with these bitter words, the indignant god leaves the desperately unhappy girl and returns home to Aphrodite, full of rage.

As I pursued Psyche's knife, patiently listening and watching this living image reveal itself, I developed an uncanny sense that the knife welcomed attention. I began to wonder if our female ancestors were more familiar with sharp blades, and more ferocious when aroused, than any written history had acknowledged. As my curiosity grew I felt myself to be in the hands of a sure, intelligent, and bemused guide. I became intrigued about the genealogy of Psyche's knife, because if it truly was a living image, then it must have kin. (Since then, I've noticed the clannish nature of images—they tend to cluster together in self-organizing groups.) The "family" to which Psyche's knife belongs in Apuleius's novel includes the lamp, Psyche, Eros, and Aphrodite, but who were the knife's ancestors? I wanted to go back into the prehistory of the Mediterranean area and search pictorial records of other ancient cultures for images of a woman with a knife.[25]

My first efforts to find an armed female in ancient history led me to mythology. Some archaeologists, anthropologists, and scholars of religion and mythology find eloquent evidence of goddess-centered traditions in the ancient world. In the absence of written records, these traditions come down to us as a "vast body of symbols preserved in the artifacts themselves" that includes rings, seals, pottery, and paintings (Gimbutas 1989, xv). The interpretation is equivocal, as classical scholars remind us, because we cannot say with any certainty what an ancient cultured believed. Authors such as Joseph Campbell, Marija Gimbutas, Erich Neumann, Marion Woodman, Edward Whitmont, Anne Baring, and Jules Cashford find strong evidence of a Great Goddess. Others, such as Elizabeth Vandiver, are far more cautious, although Vandiver (2001) does discuss clear textual evidence for particular goddesses. A decade ago I was wholeheartedly in the Great Goddess camp, but now I find myself uncomfortably in the middle, not entirely persuaded that she existed for ancient peoples around the world. I wonder, for instance, how much our modern re covery of a single Great Goddess is part of the persistent tendency toward monotheistic belief that has developed over the last five millennia, producing the idea of a single god variously imagined as Yahweh, Adonai, Jesus, and Allah. Is it possible that the idea of a single Great Goddess who in herself unites the many facets of individual female divinities is another manifestation of this monotheistic tendency?

The question then becomes, what is the value and meaning of a single god or goddess as opposed to a polytheistic approach? How does it reflect this moment in human history?

I am, however, convinced of this: the contemporary belief in an ancient Great Goddess has important psychological meaning now, a modern myth that we need for reasons we probably don't fully understand. She is an archetypal experience emerging out of the deep layers of the objective psyche, self-organizing into a meaningful pattern at this moment in history. For women and for men she appears spontaneously in dreams and artwork, in stories and films, and in visions and rituals. Surely this has something to do with the need shared by both men and women to redefine female and feminine—a key concern of this book—in part through seeking an original female archetype who gives us a sense of femininity's grandeur. So regardless of her prehistory, today the Great Goddess has become a symbol of "the life force in matter," "the paradox at the heart of reality," and "the energy we need to become whole" (Woodman and Dickson 1997, 3, 38, and 51). The power of the Great Goddess is "a woman's natural domain" and a realm of experience that grants authority and wisdom (Schwartz-Salant 1982, 100).[26]

I'm not immune to the seductive power of seeking the original female, the one I want to claim as ancestor in part because of her fierceness. It was thrilling to read this passage from Edward Whitmont:

> The oldest deities of warfare and destruction were feminine, not masculine. Listen to their all but forgotten names: Inanna in Sumer, Anath in Canaan, Ishtar in Mesopotamia, Sekhmet in Egypt, the Morrigan in Eir, Kali in India, Pallas in Greece, and Bellona in Rome. These archaic goddesses had dominion over both love and war. They were credited with both chastity and promiscuity, nurturing motherliness and bloodthirsty destructiveness. But they were not at all concerned with conquest and territorial expansion. Those were male obsessions. Rather, these goddesses monitored the life cycle throughout its phases: birth, growth, love, death, and rebirth. (1982, viii)

It seemed to me then, when I first discovered these startling images, just as it seems to me now, a decade later, that a necessary step in reimagining female grandeur is reimagining the range of female power. A grand female is a powerful female. This search for ancestors was a search on behalf of my self and my many sisters whose lack of power crippled our lives. I did not, and do not, want to pass on this crippling legacy to others. Is it any wonder that Psyche's knife would speak to me?

As I went back into Mediterranean prehistory seeking an ancestor for Psyche's knife, I didn't find a knife exactly, but something else just as intriguing: the Minoan serpent goddess who wields a double-edged ax.

The Double-headed Ax of the Goddess

On the island of Crete 1,500 years before Apuleius wrote "Eros and Psyche," the people we now call Minoan, after legendary King Minos, inhabited a rich culture that continued to flourish long after other Mediterranean civilizations had eroded.[27] One of the most exquisite Minoan artifacts is a small statue of a goddess who holds a serpent in each outstretched hand, as though she is displaying them to an assembled audience. She's come to be known as the Cretan (or Minoan) serpent goddess. In other artifacts, the serpent goddess holds a double-headed ax, a flat blade with two sharp edges shaped something like butterfly wings attached to a sturdy shaft. Sometimes the ax appears by itself without the goddess, but it never appears alongside male figures (Baring and Cashford 1991, 114). For example, in the western wing of the great palace at Knossos on Crete, pillars in the main area and in the subterranean vaults are decorated with images of the double ax. In addition, tall bronze-headed axes, some two meters high, stood on either side of the altar to the goddess (Gimbutas 1989, 223).[28]

Anthropologists and mythologists who read these ancient images believe that the double-headed ax symbolizes the serpent goddess. The ax is part of her iconography in the same way that the cross, for example, is associated with Jesus of Nazareth. Just as the cross has numerous associations pointing toward the deeper meaning of Christ for modern Christians, the ax probably had great spiritual significance for the Minoan people. We'll never know with any certainty what it meant to them nearly three millennia ago, but we can dream the myth onward and ask, What could a goddess wielding a sharp ax mean today? One obvious answer is death and rebirth, for two reasons. First, the crypts on Knossos are thought to represent the womb of the Minoan goddess where the "transformation from death to life took place and where initiation rites were performed" (Gimbutas 1989, 223). Second, the Minoan goddess is shown holding two serpents, a creature that symbolizes transformation because of its ability to shed its own skin.[29]

Discovering the Minoan serpent goddess with her double-headed ax opened up an entire world of uncannily similar images that predate the Minoan culture by as much as 50,000 years. For instance, the ax has been found in Paleolithic excavations, an era that extends from 50,000 to 10,000 BCE, specifically the cave of Niaux in southwestern France. Axes also have been discovered during excavations of the Tell Halaf in modern-day Iraq, a Neolithic site built sometime between 10,000 and 3,500 BCE (Baring and Cashford 1991, 112). At these and other ancient sites in Greece, Bulgaria, Yugoslavia, and southeastern Italy, beautifully made greenstone axes, tiny in size, have been found (Gimbutas 1989, 290). They are called "cultic axes" to distinguish them from axes that may have been tools or weapons because the materials used to fashion these double axes, including gold and thin sheets of bronze as well as soft stone, make them unsuitable for utilitarian use.

As a ritual object, the double-headed ax associates the Minoan serpent goddess with ceremonial or symbolic death, but not necessarily with warfare.[30] Yet by arguing that the ax of the goddess is only a ritual object—unlike a warrior's ax, which is truly and horribly lethal—we run the risk of negating its power. This line of reasoning also bespeaks a naïve understanding of ritual. Transformative rituals, in which one is initiated into a new role within the culture, often involve severe suffering and sacrifice if not actual bloodshed. According to Victor Turner, the experience "is frequently likened to death, to being in the womb, to invisibility, to darkness, to bisexuality, to the wilderness, and to an eclipse of the sun or moon" (quoted in Mahdi, Foster, and Little 1987, 95). Any one of these experiences can be frightening. Combined, they may terrify, which is partly the point. Those undergoing the ritual are stripped of their comforting surround, a move that is intentionally humbling and disorienting, to prepare them for what's to come. "It is as though the initiates are being reduced or ground down to a uniform condition to be fashioned anew" (ibid.).

If we stop to think about the actual ordeal of effective ritual, I think we would be less tempted to take the ax of the goddess lightly. Minimizing the lethal potential of the ax as weapon or as symbol can lead to an overly tender view of goddesses, females, and the feminine. I am loathe to split the domains along rigid lines of sex and gender wherein males, both human and divine, wield battle-axes with bloody consequences while females, both human and divine, use axes in polite ceremony and as part of the palace décor. If we draw these lines, we may as well stop right here and say that Psyche didn't really mean to use a knife.

The Butterfly of the Goddess

In seeking an ancestor to Psyche's knife, I discovered an interesting resemblance between the double ax and the butterfly, another image of transformation associated with ancient goddesses.[31] Images of the butterfly found in Czechoslovakian frescoes and pottery from the 5th millennium, for example, are visual prototypes of the Minoan double ax—almost as though the craftspeople used the same schematic to create both! As iron battle-axes became more prominent in the second millennium BCE, the double head of the ritual ax began to resemble the butterfly more and more, perhaps to maintain a symbolic meaning that had little to do with warfare.[32] We'll never know for sure, but we can speculate that the butterfly represented the idea "that there were two aspects to a single life-form: one was 'born' out of the other. Like the serpent, the butterfly became one of the oldest images to suggest the regeneration of life from an outworn form. It also took on an additional meaning, the survival of the soul after the death of the body" (Baring and Cashford 1991, 73).[33] Since that time, the butterfly has symbolized the souls of the dead, the souls of dreamers wandering through other worlds (Gimbutas 1989, 245), and a manifestation of the breath of life, the divine soul that animates matter (Johnson 1988, 194).

In the gardens outside my office, I often see beautiful monarch butterflies elegantly floating among the plants and flowers. The words of Lionel Corbett come back to me:

> It is no accident that in antiquity the butterfly used to symbolize the soul, or that "psyche" originally meant breath—both of these evoke a sense of alive movement. Nowhere is the movement or the sense of the life of the psyche seen more clearly than in story, which moves images and affects towards a satisfying end that resonates within us. Sacred story, or myth . . . conveys critically important knowledge about creation, life, and death. (1996, 85)

Psyche's story is a living myth that conveys critically important knowledge, including the paradoxical idea that proximity to death can intensify our feeling of life—and that transformation epitomizes this proximity. Watching the butterflies on any given day, although I am surprised and delighted, I rarely give a thought to what they endured to become butterflies. Yet my remote ancestors, "equipped with only the patience to observe, recognized all the stages of the drama and incorporated it into [their] symbolism at least seven or eight thousand years ago" (Gimbutas 1982, 190). They knew that the monarch I watch today began its life as a caterpillar, passed through a chrysalis stage, and then emerged as this lovely winged creature completely unlike its previous self.

I pause a moment and consider this word *transformation*. It's often used in a blithe manner, perhaps made easier because our central symbol for transformation, the butterfly, is so delicate. We may know intellectually that transformation requires destruction and death. We probably don't know, emotionally, that "most of the caterpillar's organs . . . dissolve, and those fluids . . . help the tiny wings, eyes, muscles and brain of the developing butterfly to grow" (Woodman 1985, 13). We also seldom remember that no other activity is possible inside that chrysalis. Literally and figuratively the caterpillar is consumed alive by transformation. Instead, we have beautiful butterflies, an image of the outcome, not the ordeal. But few people who have been through the ordeal of transformation can forget the grinding, exhausting, horrible pain of the experience. They rarely take the word *transformation* lightly.

In fact, we're fortunate to have an alternative to the delicate butterfly as a symbol of transformation. The double-bladed ax of the goddess is as ancient as the butterfly and as feminine in its organic understanding of death-in-life. It also is more potent because, like the famous sword of Damocles, which hung by thin thread over his head, the ax of the goddess carries with it the real threat of an unknown and unknowable fate. When will the blade strike? What will it strike? And what life will emerge from this death? At a feeling level, where hearts are broken and loss is abysmal, the double ax is a more apt symbol of the real trauma of transformation. This is especially true for the person in the midst of it, "waiting for the ax to fall"—an interesting vestige in language—and those who are still shuddering from its sharp edge. In the midst of profound transformation, the final form our lives will take is not yet manifest, nor is life itself guaranteed. All we know is that "for life to proceed and renew itself, it must also be destroyed; joyous living and painful destruction are mutually interdependent and need each other" (Whitmont 1982, 56).

The interdependence of creation and destruction and the ecstasy of life and death are key themes in the tale of Eros and Psyche, particularly during the confrontation when Psyche's knife is literally present. Psyche's willingness to destroy the original relationship with Eros permits the creation of a new relationship between the lovers. In considering the ax as an ancestor to Psyche's knife, we gain an archetypally feminine perspective on this pivotal moment, the perspective of death-in-life. This is a wise alternative to the more conventional idea that the knife symbolizes the animus of Psyche's sisters who speak as the "man-hating voices of the matriarchy" (Downing 1988, 49).

If the presiding deity in this moment is a goddess with her sacrificial ax, then we need to look at Psyche's action with new eyes. She uses the lamp and the knife not simply in wanton, aggressive destruction for its own sake. Psyche isn't motivated to destroy her lover at all, unless of course he truly is a monster. Psyche's knife is an agent of transformation and her gesture is for the sake of new life. We are like Psyche in those moments when "we agree to let go of one style of loving in order to affirm another. The loss, of course, is real—else it would not be a sacrifice. But the new life which we affirm through sacrifice is real as well" (Mogenson 1992, 47). Like Psyche, we act largely in the dark and it's risky, as I suggested at the end of chapter 2. Yet when we are guided by longing for a whole and more truthful relationship to the beloved and to ourselves, not acting is the greater risk.

Doubling, Dualism, and Wholeness

Marie-Louise von Franz asserts that there is an "ultimate instinct of truth in the human psyche which, in the long run, cannot be suppressed" (1980, 94). This instinct for truth is embodied in the classical Jungian idea of the Self, the archetype of wholeness, which we can think of as both a guide and the goal (1928, par. 399). Though no one ultimately reaches the Self, the continual striving toward it produces greater consciousness of our whole character, the shadows as well as the light. Could Psyche's knife symbolize this aim? Very likely, because it has two sharp edges, not one.

The number two and the idea of the pair or doubling are characteristic of ancient artifacts associated to goddess figures. Notice that the ax is double-edged and the butterfly has a pair of wings. The number two is also considered feminine in such symbol systems as the Tarot, in which the Popess (*La Papesse*) or High Priestess is number two in the Major Arcana.[34] Twoness or doubling doesn't suggest that a goddess is dualistic but rather that she is multifaceted and therefore whole. Moreover, wholeness has long been considered an attribute of the archetypal feminine, not the masculine with its associations to singleness, single-mindedness, and linearity.[35] Therefore we might conjecture that Psyche's double-edged knife expresses the intrinsic wholeness of the soul and serves as a timely reminder not to view her in only one way. She is not merely poor, simple Psyche, a tenderhearted and naïve young girl. She also is an intuitive woman who heeds the creative urge toward wholeness and a bold woman who faces her lover with a lamp and knife to discover the truth, however monstrous it may be.

As a guiding psychological principle, doubling and dualism call to mind the old adage, "there are always two sides to every story." In fact, every story is many-sided. We can fully appreciate this when we use any character, including the setting, as an entry point for our imagination into a story and avoid limiting ourselves to a single, fixed perspective. Talented storytellers know this: many successful novels, plays, and films have been marvelous retellings of classic tales from another point of view, for instance, Gregory Maguire's *Wicked* or John Gardner's empathetic retelling of the Beowulf legend, *Grendel*. Shifting perspective doesn't merely tell the other side. It opens up the entire narrative to many different insights. For instance, the two different stories that Psyche tells her sisters about her unseen lover make them justifiably suspicious. Psyche herself seems embarrassed about not keeping her story straight and rushes her sisters out of the palace with heaps of valuable gems as though to buy their complicity. It doesn't work. At that time, I doubt Psyche realized that this one mistake, this small crack in the façade of her perfect existence where the stories didn't hold together, would initiate such a profound transformation. It opened up everything.

I recall the first time I realized that transformation can begin with a barely perceptible separation, a separation that, over time, opens up into an abyss. As youngsters, my brother and I would pile into a neighbor's station wagon along with a bunch of other rambunctious kids to ride down the steep hill to our elementary school. One morning as we made the left onto Chelton, we felt, and heard, a bump. I remember looking back to see a small crack in the asphalt road behind us, then I turned around in my seat and continued chattering with my friend, thinking nothing of it. The next morning when we came to the crack, the bump was a sharp, loud thump. The crack now extended across the entire two-lane road. I shivered. Over the course of the school day I continued to feel that sharp thump in my whole body.

The next morning we turned left onto Chelton and slowed way down. All of us stopped talking and held our breath as the car rolled slowly forward. Thump, thump! The crack was now a ledge, with the road downhill from the crack at least six inches lower. I stared through the back window: the asphalt looked like a thick layer of black frosting over a golden brown cake. Then my gaze flicked to the right. The "metal monster"—our nickname for the brand new home built entirely of steel, concrete, and glass just across the street—seemed to have a front row seat to the drama unfolding on its doorstep. Later, I would realize front row seats aren't always a good thing.

As it turned out, a water main had broken under the street. The tiny crack we barely noticed that first day was just the beginning of a process that destroyed a hundred feet of street, two homes, and part of a third. I remember this vividly because we watched, day by day, as the upright steel girders of the metal monster, huge as tree trunks, simply folded up like flimsy paper, bursting the plate glass walls and tilting the concrete floors at a terrifying angle. At first I thought it was the slowness that mesmerized me. Now I think it was the inevitability. One small crack and nothing would be the same again.

Separation marks the beginning of change, a small or large shift that we can feel in our entire body. It is essential to the psychological process of becoming since "it is only separation, detachment, and agonizing confrontation that produce consciousness and understanding" (Jung and Kerenyi 1951, 125). The first small crack for Psyche, as I mentioned before, occurred long before she prepared the lamp and sharpened the knife because by then the gap had already opened to an irreparable degree. It occurred even before her keen and malicious sisters witnessed Psyche's two conflicting stories. I imagine the crack originated in an innocent impulse—to visit with her sisters. When Psyche invited them into her private world, she may have known at some deeply unconscious level that they would see things that she did not. We often need others to see and hear a situation differently, and to help us see and hear ourselves differently, because often we do know the truth—we just don't know that we know it. Friends and especially enemies can reveal uncomfortable truths by mirroring back to us the shadowy aspects of our character.

Philosophers and artists have long known that each single person is, in fact, a whole world of diverse persons. It's become a core idea in archetypal psychology. When an experience cracks us open—just like the street in my old neighborhood—it gives us a new view of what is beneath the surface. Then we realize that becoming whole is not a question of achieving unity, it is in recognizing our actual diversity, "a process of differentiating, of differing, of recognizing the many complexes, voices, and persons that we each are" (Hillman 1983, 66). Separation and recognition of what must be separated are key, whether the separated parts form opposites or opposition is simply one kind of relationship possible between two things. Moreover, even if we aim at unity in our psychological development, we must remember the lesson of alchemy: only separated things can unite. We see this in Psyche's story by examining her two marriages, the first a semblance of marriage in Eros's golden palace achieved through abduction and seduction and the second a sacred union witnessed by all the gods on Mount Olympus. Alchemy teaches us that the first marriage, a lesser *coniunctio*, had to dissolve to make way for the second marriage, the true and sacred *heiros gamos*.

Like Psyche, many people may find that their first marriage is too confining. It becomes a prison constructed in part by the effort to be perfect. The more the ground below the relationship begins to slip sideways—and as who they have vowed to be and who they actually are start to diverge—the greater the strain to appear perfect. This strain is particularly acute if they are attempting to live up to a rigidly proscribed ideal that has been defined by culture, class, or religion. They barely know how exhausting it is until the surface cracks. This may be when the soul's instinct for truth demands a painful sacrifice—the sacrifice of perfection in the service of wholeness. This may be where Psyche's knife is the direct descendent of the goddess's double-headed ax.

Strategies to Diminish Females and the Feminine

Scholars who study ancient religions note that in the oldest traditions one goddess frequently presides over several distinct functions—a goddess of fertility and abundance is also a goddess of war, for instance—and embodies many different, possibly conflicting, characteristics, qualities, and emotions, such as benevolence and rage. Miriam Robbins-Dexter (1990) aptly refers to such goddesses as transfunctional. Joseph Campbell describes the Goddess as all-embracing and universal, a divinity who is "bisexual, absolute, and single in her generative role" (1991, 63, 66). Erich Neumann also emphasizes the androgyny of the Goddess. In painting and sculpture, she is frequently "equipped with a phallus and sometimes a beard . . . symbolizing the unity of the creative in the primordial Creatrix" (Neumann 1956, 12). The most ancient goddesses are the most whole. Psychologically, they are complex, comprised of multiple ways of being and playing multiple roles.

Today, we can scarcely grasp the wholeness expressed in a female figure with breasts, a beard, and a phallus because we have been "left with particularized or minimized goddesses" in the last few millennia (Perera 1981, 19). We have been so thoroughly socialized to split the masculine and the feminine that it seems bizarre. The phallus and beard appear prosthetic—artificial devices females adopt to borrow the powers of a male. They seem to call attention to what is lacking instead of reminding us of the androgynous potency of an aptly named Great Goddess. As unconscious Freudians, in fact, we may assume that a goddess with beard and a phallus is a frustrated female, probably sneaky or deceitful, attempting to acquire by stratagem unnatural power or status. A phallic woman, whether divine or mortal, is now perceived as an immature or distorted example of so-called normal female development. We inherit this view from Freud, who himself unfortunately tended toward the simplistic and literal in his views of women. But he is not alone. Men and women throughout history have colluded in two primary strategies to diminish females and femininity, with dire consequences for all of us. First, we have imagined females as naturally passive. Second, we have imagined females as naturally peaceful and, therefore, morally superior to males. Of the two, the second is most insidious. But both are dangerously reductive, a cage from which I hope someday we can release ourselves.

The Passive Feminine

Let's first investigate a woman's so-called natural passivity. In Freud's theories of childhood development, the phallic stage for a young girl is the third and penultimate developmental phase before she faces the shattering realization that she is castrated. When little girls successfully pass through the third stage of development, they acknowledge their physical deficiency—no penis—and renounce activity for passivity to become fully feminine. "Passivity now has the upper hand," Freud says, "which clears the phallic activity out of the way [and] smoothes the ground for femininity" (Freud 1933, 157–161). Freud's recipe for a woman's psychological health—to be appropriately female is to be fully feminine is to be passive—is the antithesis of psychological wholeness, which asserts that a wide array of femininities and masculinities is possible and healthy for women—just as for men.

Although it might be tempting to react strongly to Freud's language, it is important to choose how to read him, either literally or symbolically. Freud's description of what it is to be phallic, for example, has many layers of meaning. At the level of individual psychology, it means to be active and initiating rather than passive and accepting. At the level of physiology, it means to be energetic and aggressive. At the level of anatomy, it means to have a penis. It's very tempting to conclude that to be phallic is to be male—once again confusing biological sex (male or female) with sociocultural gender (masculine and feminine). It has taken decades of bold and careful feminist thinking to differentiate sex from gender, to see that "gender is produced primarily not by individual choices, but, more fundamentally, by social structures and their culturally distinctive meanings" (Harding 1996, 435). If gender is a production, then it is also a process—fluid, dynamic, and protean, not fixed or rigid. It changes over time, it is different from culture to culture, and it shows up among ordinary people in distinctive ways. Although phallic power is archetypally masculine, there is absolutely nothing that prevents any woman from expressing it; it is part of our common human inheritance.[36]

But how many of us really are Freudians? W. H. Auden, in his encomium to Freud, says it nicely: Freud was not so much an individual man as he was a whole climate of opinion (2007, 100). Just about anyone born or educated in twentieth- and twenty-first-century Europe or North America lives in this climate of opinion. Considering the aggressive spread of Western culture and values to almost all parts of the world, especially through the media and consumerism, many non-Western countries have been exposed to this climate of opinion too. Most of us are more Freudian than we realize. One of the significant ways this shows up is the belief that power and potency are expressed through activity and that, as a result, they are exclusively phallic and masculine.

This legacy clearly affects how we as women and men see ourselves and our capacities. When we accept Freud's assumption
that passivity is natural to the feminine, the cost becomes all too
apparent. It permits humanity to fit female and the feminine into
a small space that reflects none of the original complexity and
wholeness of goddess figures from any number of traditions—
along with none of their power and none of the weighty responsibility that arises from that power. Femininity can no longer
be limited this way, says Jungian scholar Edward Whitmont. "It
will discover and express its active, initiating, creative, and transformative capacity . . . the readiness to demand and challenge"
(1982, 189). Psyche, knowingly or not, was ready to demand and
challenge. She is an example of the original power of an ancient
goddess working through the actions of a vulnerable and confused girl who is unwilling to remain passive another night.

Women's hunger for a more active and potent spirituality—
one with a female taking her rightful place at the center of her
own story—drives the contemporary movement to rediscover the
Great Goddess. Millions of women from all spiritual traditions
imagine her as a mentor and guide toward a whole femininity.
Collectively, we are creating a new myth centered on the sacred
feminine. She is a psychological necessity.

When we resort to gender stereotyping and confuse biological sex with sociocultural gender, we see "discrimination against
women, primarily, where we must deal with a repression of femininity in women and men" (Whitmont 1982, 127). The result is
that Western men and women have been forced to make their
way in a world that has degraded and demonized the feminine
which, as an archetype, is fully available to and embodied in both
sexes. Richard Tarnas's epilogue to his study of Western philo-
sophical development eloquently describes the historical denigra-
tion of the feminine:

> It has been from start to finish an overwhelming
> masculine phenomenon. The "man" of the Western
> tradition has been a questing masculine hero, a Pro-
> methean biological and metaphysical rebel who has
> constantly sought freedom and progress for himself.
> [This evolution] has been founded on the repression of

the feminine—on the repression of . . . mystery and ambiguity, of imagination, emotion, instinct, body, nature, woman. (1991, 441–42)

Tarnas conjectures that the splitting of masculine and feminine, though largely an unconscious phenomenon, was a necessary creative step in Western history. For example, the ongoing process of differentiation in the life of an individual—which includes everything from cell mitosis to establishing an identity within the family to sorting through one's mature preferences, beliefs, and values—is characteristic of creation. Yet was the win-lose approach inherent in the domination of masculine over feminine truly necessary? Is it possible to make distinctions without creating winners and losers? We can imagine it, with difficulty, and we must imagine it if we are to transform culture. To begin, though, we must face the reality that the feminine has been repressed— and examine all of the overt and subtle ways in which this is embedded in our thinking and feeling. If we don't, we will create a flawed and incomplete foundation for going forward, one as damaging as the original repression of the feminine.

To return to my theme of the passive feminine, going forward includes staying alert to the ways we continue to be unconscious Freudians. When we recoil even slightly from a woman's boldness, courage, directness, or ferocity, when we judge it as abnormal or think she's acting like a man, we're guilty of equating "female" with "passive." We're also guilty of diminishing the feminine as a mode of being equally available to men and women.

The Peaceful Feminine

Sociologist Riane Eisler confidently explains why creating a hierarchy occurred in the wake of splitting the masculine and the feminine and encourages us to enlarge our imagination of history to include examples of peaceful coexistence alongside the plentiful examples of conquest and bloodshed. Eisler asserts that ancient people who worshipped the Great Goddess were organized into partnership societies that expressed feminine values. They were overthrown by waves of nomadic warriors, dominator societies wherein masculine values prevailed and the power of the blade was worshipped. The feminine chalice and the masculine blade symbolize the two kinds of power. The blade is "the power to take away or to dominate" whereas the chalice is "the power to nurture and to give" (Eisler 1987, 48, 28). In discussing our evolution toward a dominator worldview, Eisler says, "Certainly the main instrument for the dramatic shift in our cultural evolution was the Blade" (76). She is careful not to ignore the double ax of the Minoan serpent goddess but interprets it as a tool that symbolized fruitfulness since it was "shaped like the hoe axes used to clear the land for the planting of crops" (36).

Eisler's interpretation of the Minoan serpent goddess's double ax is a case in point of the subtle ways in which the repressed feminine is embedded in our Freudian thinking. The ax of the goddess, she is saying, isn't really an ax; it's not really and truly sharp, dangerous, or lethal. It is not like the axes men use because only males resort to violence and bloodshed to achieve power over others; women resort to violence and bloodshed only when they become enchanted with the masculine dominator agenda. This is an old idea in a new wrapper: the claim to moral superiority that feminists used a century ago. Eventually feminists realized that it is dishonest to simultaneously assert superiority and strive for equality. Either females are morally pure or we are fully human—one or the other. Idealizing females and the feminine as nurturing, bountiful, and peaceful—that is, pretending we are not equally capable of violent, aggressive, and controlling behavior as any male—is not merely naïve. It's boring. Likewise, it is naïve to ignore the violent and destructive potential of any sharp blade, double-edged dagger, or double-headed ax, no matter who it belongs to. As the numerous stories of ferocious and well-armed goddesses and heroines attest, the bounds of female power greatly exceed the rules of polite society.

Scholars have faithfully interpreted evidence of an alternate model of social organization that tended to be more agrarian and cooperative than nomadic and aggressive. The art and artifacts suggest it and reasoned imagination supports it. Generally speaking, the set of skills and characteristics required for humanity to establish its territory is different from the skills needed to cultivate that territory. This difference is historical, sociological, and archetypal. In the novel *Lavinia*, Ursula Le Guin's imaginative account of Aeneas's princess bride, she says that Mars (the Roman god of war) lives at the edges of the fields because the same people who spend months and years cultivating their crops will be called upon to defend them. Ploughshares and swords both are necessary to preserve the life of a community. Any person, male or female, might feel the pull of home and partnership at one moment and the need to expand, explore, and conquer at another. Odysseus, weary at the end of the Trojan War, longed to return home to Penelope. Amelia Earhart, born in a time and place that imagined female fulfillment in the safe confines of the home, longed for the risky adventure of flight in the early years of aeronautics.

If we are going to project our longing for a more peaceful new age onto the past, and specifically onto one group from the past, let's be honest about it. Even better, let's not, and instead try to appreciate the true complexity of gender roles, because we all pay a steep price when we imagine one domain or impulse as typically feminine, female, and womanly and another as masculine, male, and manly. Would we really have any of the dynamic, powerful women in industry and politics—to name just two arenas where women have shown their mettle—if women had no instinct for conquest and no idea how to go for the throat when necessary? Stereotyping widens the political and sociocultural divide between women and men. It does not provide a holistic vision of human potential, which includes our shared capacity for violence, bloodshed, and destruction. Nor is it a healing vision for our shared future, a healing which can begin only when we tell the truth about ourselves.

The Fierce Female across Cultures

When we feel awe and fear at the lethal potential of the goddess's double ax, we gain a more realistic sense of her power. Archaeological evidence from the island of Crete and from Old Europe gives us a few images of the fierce feminine. She also appears in many other traditions, perhaps as an ancestral expression of the same urge that inspired Psyche to take up the lamp and sharpen her knife. Below I offer a sample of these fierce females, those who particularly speak to me because they fed my imagination of the whole feminine. They include the Hindu goddesses Durga and Kali; Judith, the Jewish heroine who decapitated Holofernes to save her people; Neith, one of the most ancient Egyptian deities; Elizabeth I of England; and Éowyn from J. R. R. Tolkien's *Lord of the Rings* trilogy. I hope this small sample serves as a potent antidote to the diminished, restricted, superficial feminine.

The Hindu Goddesses Durga and Kali

In classical Hindu mythology, the goddess Durga is one of the many manifestations of the Great Goddess (Mahadevi), who has many names and appears in many different forms. This plurality, as we have seen in other traditions, is one way of expressing the power and pervasiveness of the goddess's realm. Durga is important for our story as an armed woman who rides into battle to behead a demon. According to the Puranas, the sacred Hindu texts from the classical period that are about 2,000 years old—contemporaneous with the Roman tale "Eros and Psyche"—Durga was created for the express purpose of killing.

The story goes that the gods, oppressed by a buffalo demon, appealed to Vishnu and Shiva to save them. The anger of Vishnu and Shiva, combined with the pent-up rage of the other gods, united in a single stream of energy that poured forth into the world and took the form of Durga. She is rage personified and bent on revenge. Then the gods bestowed on this fearsome goddess the tools and weapons she would use to confront the demon, including the lion that carried her into battle. Durga is typically portrayed astride a lion, her expression serene and confident. In her multiple arms (she usually has four or eight of them), she holds a variety of implements, including a trident, a thunderbolt, a sword, and a dagger. In at least one thirteenth-century painting, Durga's weapons also included a serpent (Patton 2007, 700). She is rather well-armed.

Hindu goddesses appear in many forms, some tender, others terrifying. Durga, a goddess of life and death, clearly takes one of the terrifying forms. As we might expect, Durga is related to another terrifying Hindu goddess, Kali, who is the fierce black goddess of death and destruction—including the relentless, destructive aspect of time since *kali* is the feminine form of the

Sanskrit word for time. Two stories about Kali are worth hearing. According to one, Durga gave birth to Kali in the midst of battling the two demons Chanda and Munda when a stream of Durga's divine rage coalesced to form her daughter. In the second story, the goddess Parvati—intent on destroying a demon—transformed herself into Kali from some poison stored in the throat of the god Shiva. "Kali acts as Parvati's alter ego, the embodiment of the cosmic power of destruction" (Rose 2007, 829). Thus either poison or rage was the amniotic fluid, so to speak, that infused Kali's becoming.

Another sacred Hindu text, the Devi Mahatmyam, tells how Kali used her ferocity to protect humans. She discovered a gigantic demon, Raktabija, who was devouring humans as fast as they were created. Swinging her sword, Kali cut the demon in two with one swing. As the drops of demon blood splatter the ground, each one became a new demon. Soon, Kali was faced with a horde. She changed her tactics and began to eat the newborn demons. Then she went to the source of the evil. She turned her attention to Raktabija's bleeding body and caught each drop of blood on her tongue before it reached the ground. To finish the battle once and for all, she sucked Raktabija's lifeblood and prevailed.

Although Kali also has a pleasing form, she is rarely shown in a tranquil or tender state. It is as though the circumstances of her birth dictate her ferocious character—which may temporarily subside but never fully disappears. In most paintings, Kali is black or dark blue, a color associated with the void or abyss from which all created things arise, including delusions. As a goddess, Kali is "beyond both fear and ignorance" and so worshippers invoke her for protection from fear and the gift of compassion and awareness (Rose 2007, 829). She is a fierce guardian and "a crusader against evil" in two ways, fighting "the evil of illusion or the more concrete evils of attackers or demons" (Patton 2007, 699).

Like the Minoan serpent goddess holding the double-edged ax, Durga and Kali present fierce images of archetypal femininity that give us a little more to think about when we ponder Psyche holding a razor-sharp dagger. As we recall how Eros kept Psyche in the dark—about his identity, about their life together—it is poetic justice to discover Kali, the destroyer of illusions. Kali reminds us that illusion is evil, requiring skill and courage to confront.

Another fierce female who has been popular as an artistic subject for hundreds of years is Judith, the heroine of the Hebrew people. Biblical accounts describe her as a "virtuous, pious, and beautiful widow" who boldly stepped into a leadership role at a crucial moment, saving the Jews from impending massacre.

The story begins with the Jews living in the Assyrian empire ruled by King Nebuchadnezzar shortly after being released from their Babylonian captivity. They had refused to aid the king in his most recent battle, so Nebuchadnezzar ordered his commander to punish the rebels. The commander, Holofernes, invaded the Jewish settlements, destroyed their sanctuaries, and proclaimed that his king, King Nebuchadnezzar, should from this day forward be worshipped as god. The Jews refused and prepared for war.

Holofernes besieged the town of Bethulia. The Jewish settlers were on the brink of surrendering when the widow Judith stepped forward and convinced her people to delay five days. It isn't clear from the text whether or not Judith had prepared a strategy or what was going through her mind. Was she angry and aroused, determined to avenge the Jews? Was she in such despair from the recent death of her husband that sacrificing her own life on a risky adventure appealed to her? Nonetheless she acted. She stripped off her widow's mourning, left Bethulia, and entered Holofernes's camp. She was brought before him, a captive. Again, we don't know what transpired next, but four days later Holofernes decided to seduce the beautiful widow and sent for Judith.

Perhaps as a result of Judith's wiles, the commander drank a great deal more wine than he should have and fell into a drunken stupor. Perhaps he never suspected a mere woman could be a threat. This is what we would call dangerously naïve. In any event, Judith acted swiftly. She cut off Holofernes's head with a sharp sword, returned to Bethulia, and with the help of her people, set it on a spike outside the city walls for all to see. When the Assyrian soldiers realized Judith had murdered their commander, the tables were turned. They disbanded and, no longer the predators, became the prey, pursued by the Jews. During Judith's long lifetime—she apparently lived to the fine old age of 105—and for a long time after her death, the Assyrians never again threatened the Jews.

Images of Judith slaying Holofernes show a beautiful, heroic widow firmly grasping his sword. The weapon is not absent, cleverly hidden, or minimized, as in depictions of Psyche with her knife. I suspect this is due to the moral simplicity of Judith's situation. Judith is acting on behalf of her tribe, Holofernes's behavior has established him as the enemy, and the situation is urgent. Psyche's situation is far more ambiguous. Her adversary is her husband and a god, Psyche's life is not literally at stake, and neither is the life of their unborn child. Furthermore Psyche, unlike the widow Judith, is characterized as a naïve and tender girl, which makes it more difficult to imagine her with a sharp blade. Yet I imagine the tender Psyche is heir to Judith's archetypal courage and ferocity. The right combination of circumstances merely awakens it.

Neith, Warrior Goddess of the Egyptians

Neith is one of the most ancient goddesses known in Egypt and her history as well as her character is long and complex. She typifies a transfunctional goddess—one who plays many roles—who was, in addition to being a warrior goddess, also a mother goddess, a creator goddess, and a funerary goddess known for her wise counsel. Neith is often shown with a crossed arrow and bow, symbolizing either hunting or warfare, and was known as the Mistress of the Bow and Ruler of the Arrow.

Neith bears one interesting similarity to the Hindu goddess Durga, who was (among other things) a manifestation of the rage of the gods. Neith could appear as the fierce Eye of Re, the Egyptian god of the sun. In other stories, Neith created both Re and his archenemy Apophis and was credited with creating the human race.

Neith's chosen weapons, bow and arrow, also link her to an important goddess we will meet in the next chapter: Artemis, the virgin goddess of the hunt. Both Neith and Artemis express the ferocity natural to female divinities, a ferocity that women and men can reclaim as native to the feminine mode of being. One bit of evidence from popular culture that we are ready to do this is the powerful feline allure of Neytiri, the warrior princess in the 2009 film *Avatar*, mentioned in chapter 1. Her weapons? A bow with a quiver of swift arrows and a sharp dagger. A second bit of evidence is Katniss Everdeen, the compelling central character in Susanne Collins's best-selling novel *The Hunger Games*, who is old beyond her years and, at age 15, already an adept predator.

Historical and Fictional Warrior Queens

Armed females such as Durga, Kali, Judith, and Neith have aroused our particular fascination throughout history. They give us, in the words of Antonia Fraser, a special frisson; whether fear or admiration, the frisson "is undoubtedly due to the fact that woman as a whole has been seen as a pacifying force throughout history . . . hers by nature and hers in duty" (1988, 7). An armed woman directly contradicts our perception of woman—and this perception, even more than the reality, is what intrigues Fraser. She points out that we cannot wholly account for our response to an armed woman by the fact that such figures are exceptional or contradictory. Instead, she believes "there is something deep in the human spirit which finds in the image of the strong and armed woman a figure of awe" (17). That "something," I suspect, is that warrior queens and other armed females remind us of our human wholeness, which particularly has been denied to women for at least three millennia. Such wholeness naturally includes strength, aggression, domination, revenge, and violence. Although that idea is uncomfortable for some people, it does not make it any less true. Despite the fact that ferociousness has long been considered unbecoming in a woman, if not downright abnormal, women and men still find it fascinating. Is it any wonder that images of the fierce feminine are "an inspiration to women as well as a source of threat and excitement to men" (335)?

Our fascination with fierce females continues unabated in the twenty-first century, as numerous examples from literature and film attest. Two are worth mentioning here: Elizabeth I of England who, in the film *Elizabeth: The Golden Age*, is shown astride a horse on the front lines with her troops, long red hair cascading over the glittering metal of her battle armor. A second is the character of Éowyn in J. R. R. Tolkein's *Lord of the Rings* trilogy, the daughter of a king who rides fully armed into battle and who, because she is a woman, is instrumental in winning the war. Before the battle, in a poignant dialogue with the heroic Aragorn, who sees Éowyn more clearly, perhaps, than she has ever been seen, he asks, "What do you fear, lady?" "A cage," Éowyn says, "to stay behind bars, until use and old age accept them, and all chance of doing great deeds is gone beyond recall or desire." (Tolkein 1955–56, 58). Though her answer saddens him, Aragorn understands the impulse to live a purposeful life. With this clarity of seeing, and this quality of honesty, is it any wonder that Éowyn falls in love with him?

Destruction and Creation

In the masterful opening statement to Jung's last great work, *Mysterium Coniunctionis,* he says, "The factors which come together in the *coniunctio* [the union of the masculine and feminine] are conceived as opposites, either confronting one another in enmity or attracting one another in love" (1955–56, par. 1). Opposition gives substance and meaning to union. Without opposition, union is not possible. But what does this really mean at the level of day-to-day living? There must be a gap between you and what you love, a border, a frontier, a membrane comprising space, time, and matter, the core constituents of lived experience, in which you know yourself to be a separate entity. The gap may be colored by a palette of emotions, including affection or anger, longing or impatience, kindliness or resentment. As anyone who has been through a breakup or divorce knows, the real end of a relationship is marked by the emotional tranquility of indifference, not the emotional vicissitudes of love. When we feel nothing, it's truly over.

Psyche's vulnerability throughout her ordeal, the confusion of thoughts, feelings, and impulses she endures, dramatizes a profound truth about the human soul. The soul's wisdom is fully embodied, making room for a variety of conflicting ideas that a receptive, vulnerable person doesn't attempt to perfect by eliminating what doesn't fit. When we adopt the soul's perspective, we realize that the more complex the experience, the less valuable is the language of a simple opposition; which may indeed create an opposite to simplify life rather than to describe it, and still less to explore it. . . . It seems clear that a new poetic language has to evolve to allow back into consciousness a sensibility that is holistic, animistic and lunar in origin, one that explores flux, continuity and phases of alternation, offering an image not of exclusive realities, nor of final beginnings and endings, but of infinite cycles of transformation. (Baring and Cashford 1991, 675–676)

Such language, like the razor-sharp edge of a polished knife or a double-headed ax, "cut[s] things together, not apart" (Whyte 1997, 51). It destroys an original, inchoate unity such as an obese idea or belief that weighs us down to create a finely differentiated understanding. But we pay for this understanding with our feeling bodies. "Pain and delight are always closely allied for the lover" (Haule 1992, 64). Many lovers cling to the bliss of union and recoil from the pain of separation, yet we cannot stop this modulation any more than we can stop the rotation of the planet that alternately brings darkness and light.

One of Freud's great contributions to our understanding of intimate relationships was to suggest that delight and pain do not merely alternate, they coexist. Our feelings for the beloved are deeply ambivalent: we love and we hate, we are attracted and repulsed, we are tender and cruel. Even this realization requires the naked sword. If we are too caught up in the power of the love potion, we cannot perceive the true complexity of our feelings and needs, let alone acknowledge them. Without the naked blade we remain fused with the beloved, imprisoned very much as Psyche was a prisoner in the palace of Eros, unable to see and incapable of action.[37] Paradoxically, this tells us that the one kind of lover who is in dire need of the power of the blade is the one incapable of knowing this. Something else, some intuition or impulse or, as in Psyche's case, some external voice that echoes an internal need must prompt us symbolically to take up the knife.

As we discussed earlier, the drive for separation in "Eros and Psyche" comes from the feminine and specifically from the sisters. They point out that Psyche does not know her beloved, nor does her beloved know Psyche. Her concession to Eros is naïve and possibly dangerous, though he doesn't see it this way. Why would he? He literally possesses a compliant and beautiful girl-bride who adores him. Psyche's sisters, albeit envious, cruel, and hateful, "push her in the way her soul requires" (Downing 1988, 4). Her action wounds both lovers and releases both to begin their individual journeys—whether or not they wanted this outcome. It was, to borrow from the lyrics to *Phantom of the Opera*, the point of no return.

"To know and be known by our beloved, we must be in an important sense alone while we are together. Relationship moves forward by a dialogue that continually circumambulates the wound that is the secret source of our bond. Worthy opponents carry on that dialogue by remaining conscious of their unity at the level of the Self while exploring the differences in their personal needs and aspirations" (Haule 1992, 204). Psyche's gesture is destruction for the sake of a larger creative purpose: literally, the creation of psyche. This calls to mind the provocative title of Sabina Spielrein's important work, published in 1912, "Destruction as the Cause of Becoming" (see also the discussion in Kerr 1993, 501).[38] Sexuality brings death in its wake, which is revealed, for example, in images of dying in the arms of the beloved. Sexual climax, sometimes referred to as "the little death," is yet another obvious example. Sex is the experience of death because it fuses two individuals: joining as annihilation.

The applicability of Spielrein's idea to the "Eros and Psyche" myth is profound and paradoxical. On the one hand, it is apparent that the original relationship between the lovers expresses exactly the kind of fusion that Spielrein alludes to. Both Eros and Psyche live out their so-called marriage as a kind of erotic dance in darkness and sleep. The first light that enters is the glow of Psyche's lamp and the reflected light cast by Psyche's sharp knife. On the other hand, the becoming that unfolds over the course of the story hinges on the dissolution of this contained, sensual paradise. Psyche's instinct for individuality causes the destruction of that which opposed it. She resists the pull toward individual death and cuts through the sensual oblivion. Psyche's aggressive act clears the way for genuine union between worthy opponents. As such, the story offers us a glimpse of the deeper needs of intimacy. The competing obligations are intimacy with the self and intimacy with the other, union with the beloved and separation from the beloved. Such competing obligations are social in an archetypal sense: solitude is deep attention to all the persons who reside within one's psyche just as union with the beloved is deep attention to all the archetypes constellated in a marriage—one's own, one's beloved's, and those arising from the union.

"We owe God a death"

Shakespeare once said we owe God a death.[39] As I ponder the image of the goddess who, with her double ax, presides over transformation, I realize that she might put it a bit differently. We may owe the patriarchal god one death, but we owe the goddess many deaths: the symbolic death of our conscious, customary, waking identity, because she understands death-in-life. This ongoing dying and rebirth affirms that we are alive, fluid and changing, fully participating in the flow of life. It also means that if we resist the symbolic deaths that full living requires, we are bound to live a superficial life.

John Patrick Shanley, discussing his play *Doubt*, speaks about this using an earthy metaphor I think the goddess would relish:

> Each of us is like a planet. There's the crust, which seems eternal. We are confident about who we are. If you ask, we can readily describe our current state. I know my answers to so many questions, as do you. . . . Your answers are your current topography, seemingly permanent, but deceptively so. Because under that face of easy response, there is another You. And this wordless Being moves just as the instant moves; it presses upward without explanation, fluid and wordless, until the resisting consciousness has no choice but to give way.
>
> It is Doubt (so often experienced initially as weakness) that changes things. When a man feels unsteady, when he falters, when hard-won knowledge evaporates before his eyes, he's on the verge of growth. The subtle or violent reconciliation of the outer person and the

inner core often seems at first a mistake, like you've gone the wrong way and you're lost. But this is emotion just longing for the familiar. Life happens when the tectonic power of your speechless soul breaks through the dead habits of the mind. Doubt is nothing less than an opportunity to reenter the Present. (2009)

Shanley describes the soul's "tectonic power," an allusion to the capacity of the deep invisible fault lines to totally disrupt, even destroy, our comfortable and predictable life. Our comfort derives from the "dead habits of the mind" that prevent true aliveness, true presence. Shanley's words remind me that the soul has "a special relationship with death" and that death pervades "Eros and Psyche" (Hillman 1997, xvi). For instance, the oracle foretells Psyche's marriage to death. Psyche, her family, and the entire community ritualize this prediction by enacting a marriage procession that takes Psyche to the literal and symbolic edge of the known world, where she is abandoned to her fate. Death reappears in the sisters' advice to kill Eros. Psyche reluctantly agrees, preparing the lamp and sharpening the knife. After the confrontation, a hopeless Psyche continually flirts with suicide and then faces the lethal rage of Aphrodite. In Psyche's final task, she journeys into the underworld, and when she nearly succeeds, she makes the one fatal mistake that leads to a deathlike trance. In many ways, death is Psyche's familiar throughout the entire story.

The constant possibility of Psyche's destruction by her own hand or through the actions of others is a perverse measure of her creative urge toward wholeness. She is growing full of soul through suffering many symbolic deaths as she progresses from girl to maiden to lover to mother to wife. With each step, something is destroyed as well as created. The French feminist Simone de Beauvoir realized this at a precocious age. In her memoir she writes, "Suddenly the future existed; it would turn me into another being, someone who would still be, and yet no longer seem, myself. I had forebodings of all the separations, the refusals, the desertions to come, and of the long succession of my various deaths" (1959, 7).

Just as with other alchemical processes, *separatio* goes on with or without our attention. Psyche's own story teaches us that dissolution and destruction are not always consciously willed or willful activities. The truly frightening prospect is that something else, something wholly other, can direct the decomposition of a carefully composed life. We can participate in this, to be sure, by recognizing and obeying the creative urge toward wholeness. For instance, we might take a dream seriously and allow it to influence the course of our life as a friend of mine did when she turned down a job offer that looked impressive to everyone else. Or we might stop in the middle of an old, repetitive fight and tease apart the inchoate emotions at the core, trying to understand their deeper meaning. Like Psyche, we often are more embroiled than detached—simply unable to analyze with any sort of clear-eyed distance. In fact, in the midst of profound transformation, resisting symbolic death with every fiber of our being, we may share more similarities with the caterpillar and its chrysalis than it is comfortable to admit. It is the substance of our own psyche that is painfully dissolving in a world that has grown opaque to our analytical mind.

Modern technological culture does not help us face the many symbolic deaths that are part of a whole life. Instead, we have spawned entire industries in the attempt to heroically overcome death and turn back the clock, clinging to youthfulness to an obscene degree. Ernest Becker's Pulitzer Prize–winning book, *The Denial of Death*, lays bare the heroic enterprise: "Society everywhere is a living myth of the significance of human life, a defiant creation of meaning" in response to "the idea of death, the fear of it [that] haunts the human animal like nothing else" (1973, 27, xvii). We refuse to see that dying is an organic, essential, frequent part of existence. It requires a deep sense of paradox to understand that "death and existence may exclude each other in rational philosophy, but they are not psychological contraries" (Hillman 1997, 60). Symbolic death is the only thing that can open us to new life, propelling us out of one existence and into a new one, like the caterpillar whose flesh is dissolved and consumed to birth the butterfly. But there is no guarantee that it will do so. The requirement seems to be a willingness to face death and loss without repressing any of the despair or self-destructive fantasies that doing so generates.

Psyche's fate illuminates our own stories. We are the work.

Those of us who choose a soul journey will endure many, many deaths in the continuing series of transformations that shape our character because "the destruction of the soul is the counterpart of the creation of the soul" (Hillman 1972, 36). Like Psyche in her pursuit of Eros, we will experience continual *separatio*—the dissolving, decomposing, detaching, and disintegrating—and become intimate with death in the midst of life. Such a journey literally makes soul. This is characteristic of any creative work, whether that work is oneself or one's marriage, a home or a garden, a child, a book, a painting, or a business. Step by painful and joyful step, destruction and creation are our constant companions. One of the great skills in life is to recognize and welcome both of them equally and keep pace with the actual fluidity of life as you flow into another form and the world around you changes.

If Psyche had not owed the goddess many deaths, what would she have become? Would she have remained a daddy's girl, a princess, untouched and untouchable in her father's kingdom, aging physically but not emotionally or spiritually? Would she have wandered through Eros's perfect palace year in and year out, allowing an indolent malaise to spread slowly through her entire being like a deadly poison?[40] Would she have succeeded in killing herself at the river, ignoring the part of her that wanted to live? Would we even have a story, rich and terrible in its object lessons for any of us who would live a psyche-centered life?

To be a Psyche is to remember that death gives birth to life, that they are not psychologically opposed to one another. This insight is embodied in the double-bladed ax that cuts both ways. Death is not something to overcome or put behind us as quickly as possible. Paradoxically, it is something to appreciate because it profoundly shapes our values, beliefs, character, and perception. For instance, in a moving passage that describes her personal encounter with death, Christine Downing says:

> I realized that not to let myself die would be a much
> worse death. I felt . . . a kind of unending fall into noth-
> ingness, nothingness, nothingness. But I discovered
> that the more I allowed myself to fall, the less it felt like
> that. I discovered that I had never really believed that
> there is a center at the center. And that there is. It was

not at all a case of overcoming my fear, of overcoming
my fragmentation or my hurts—but precisely the
discovery that such overcoming is beside the point.
(1981, 47)

Downing and others discover the center at the center and emerge
from the experience with the darkness of death and depth in their
flesh. They have a continual reminder that they have dwelled in
the underworld for a time, the realm of the chthonic feminine
that is the soul's native habitat. Such travelers know that this experience among the dead offers tangible support—as tangible as
bone and muscle—for every living, creative endeavor. These de-
scents into depth matter, and they make a life that matters, in a
way that an uninitiated person has no feel for. Simply, they mark
the traveler with indelible dark ink. I imagine that this must be
how William Styron chose the title of his magnificent memoir of
depression: *Darkness Visible* (1990).

4

LUNAR KNIFE

*The moon crescent and the sickle-shaped sword occur repeatedly in
mythological imagery. They refer to the rising power of the feminine . . .
and the fact that the force of the moon, the force of the psychic tides
of life, of emotion rather than rational functioning,
represents an energy not to be disregarded.*
—EDWARD WHITMONT, *RETURN OF THE GODDESS*

Psyche lays on the rough stone floor of the palace, exhausted and
downcast. The draft from Eros's hasty flight chills the tears on her
cheeks to ice. She is so cold, cold like death. And then the mournful
litany begins, as steady as her heart: Eros is gone. He is gone. Love
is gone.

Time passes, though she hardly knows it except by the slow mutation
of leaden thought into agonizing questions: What have I done? Was
everything he said true? Was it? Later she remembers the prophecy, the
fates who decreed a marriage to death. They never understood it, none
of them—not even her own mother who had married, too, and should
have known, should have told her.

Psyche gets up from the floor slowly and, like a sleeper trapped in a
nightmare, walks out of the palace. There is no place to go except away,
nothing to seek except nothingness. The cool ground slopes downward
and so she stumbles forward, blind to the profusion of beauty
surrounding her: trees shining in brilliant sunlight, the soft caress of
delicate grasses that gently catch the edge of her gown as if to stop her,
the rich scent of jasmine and honeysuckle tempting her to pause and
enjoy. But there is no joy left, not for her, not in all the world.

Psyche walks on. She doesn't notice the gentle laughter of Pan and
Echo, side by side on the hill, practicing the flute—nor the sudden

silence as they watch the girl, unseeing, uncaring, already not of this world. She hears only the rush of the swift river growing steadily louder, a welcome roaring in her ears that nearly drowns out her thoughts of Eros flying away, as though it is all a dream, or a nightmare. She slips on the rocks near the riverbank and falls to her knees, then crawls over the boulders like an animal, trailing her long gown in the mud. Finally, at the river's frothy edge, she stands upright and steps into the cold, cold water.

As I descended into Psyche's story I moved steadily closer to an embodied way of knowing. Here, new knowledge can arrive in a flash, like a door to a bright room suddenly thrown open. This is the only way to explain how "Eros and Psyche," a myth dominated by the sunlit goddess Aphrodite, would reveal itself to be a rich lunar landscape pervaded by the power of Artemis. In the astonishing way of archetypes that reveal their numinous power in true opposites, it is as though Aphrodite, the soul's nemesis and teacher throughout "Eros and Psyche," conjured Artemis, the fierce virgin goddess of solitude, the wilderness, and wild animals.

It all started with a single, spontaneous gesture that released a rich insight. I had decided I wanted to buy a knife to mark the beginning of this project, something to look at over the months and years ahead. I found my knife easily: handcrafted and one of a kind, it is about seven inches long with a beautifully shaped blade and a bone handle. (Even as I write these words, a decade later, the knife I purchased sits in front of me.) When I returned to my house, I didn't see the bright sunlight streaming through the kitchen window, nor did I see that the living room was dim. I wasn't paying attention to anything at all—except the desire to take the shiny, razor-sharp blade out of its thick leather sheath. As I did, I extended my arm to the side and lifted the knife high overhead in a graceful arc, as though I was a dancer following someone else's choreography.

My eyes followed the beauty of the shining blade up, up, toward the ceiling. Then I caught something odd on the periphery of my vision. A trembling disk of light floated in mid-air, like an ethereal lamp carried by invisible hands. Mystified, it took me a few moments to realize what it was: a patch of brightness created by sunlight streaming through the window that bounced off the silver surface of the blade. Thus, in my dimly lit living room, the knife became a source of reflected light, like the moon to the sun. Without any forethought, I had enacted part of the confrontation between Psyche and Eros and discovered the lunar knife.

Let us return to the story for a moment to see the lunar quality of Psyche's knife. The sisters have told Psyche that she is sleeping with a monster who will devour her and their unborn child, and so she spends a tumultuous, emotional day trying to decide what to do. Finally, as night approaches, Psyche resolves to confront her lover. She prepares the lamp, sharpens the knife, and hides them near the bed. In the middle of the night, the room now silent and dark, they appear relaxed in each other's arms, depleted from the combats of love, but only Eros lays sleeping. Psyche remains alert and stealthily leaves his side to retrieve the lamp and knife she had prepared hours before. She raises the lamp overhead and approaches the sleeper, close enough to see him and, if necessary, to kill him.

At this moment, Psyche's lamp is the only source of light. Since a single flame could not be bright enough to completely illuminate the bedchamber, it remains shadowy and dark. This darkness, however, directs attention to the exquisite beauty of the sleeping Eros much like chiaroscuro in a painting by Rembrandt or Caravaggio directs our attention to the shapes emerging from the shadows. Chiaroscuro hints at the mystery intrinsic to any portrait: we are always more than we seem, just as Psyche in this moment is far more than a simple, compliant girl. The surrounding darkness also renders a second source of light, light reflecting the lamp's brightness, dramatically important. In the lover's private world, Psyche's lamp is the primary light source just as the sun is the primary light source for our planet. Psyche's knife, which reflects the lamp's illumination, is analogous to the moon.

The presence of a symbolic moon in this story completely surprised me. In the end, I realized that seeing beyond the powerful presence of Aphrodite, who dominates Psyche's fate, adds a rich layer to my exploration of love and power. For instance, even in Aphrodite's realm—where warmth, passion, and intimacy are cherished—a goddess of the moon in the Greek tradition, Artemis, has her place. Aphrodite conjures Artemis in the same way that a surfeit of intimacy awakens our longing for solitude. In fact, Aphrodite doesn't merely conjure Artemis, she demands Artemis. The ability to be alone while we are together, to stand on our own, apart, as a whole person, is a hallmark of true union. Artemis, a lunar goddess of the wilderness, is also clearly present after Eros has abandoned Psyche and she sees little point in living. The loss of her beloved connects Psyche to other sources of love and other kinds of solace—the consolation of living nature— where Artemis is entirely at home. And finally, Psyche's knife has an uncanny ancestor, a crescent-shaped blade called a moon weapon, symbolizing the rising power of the feminine (Whitmont 1982, 32). Let us begin with the moon weapon.

Scythe and Knife: The Rising Power of the Feminine

At the moment Psyche uses the knife, she stands at the end of one life and the beginning of another.[41] This is a dramatic moment of death-in-life, an instant within the continual cycles of life associated with feminine consciousness, the moon, and the earth, each with their unceasing cyclical change. This moment in Psyche's journey calls to mind the new moon, which is crescent shaped like a sickle or scythe used to harvest grain, and is associated with death. Once again, we see how images of birth and death are bound to one another.

The relationship between the scythe, death, and time has an intriguing origin in Greek mythology that involves incest, hatred, attempted infanticide, revenge, castration—and a linguistic mistake. Is it any wonder Freud and Jung were fascinated by antiquity? The story is one interlude in Hesiod's account of the origins of the cosmos, *Theogony*, a creation myth at the core of the Greek tradition.[42] In the beginning, so goes the myth, was Chaos and broad-breasted Gaia, misty Tartarus and Eros. Gaia, the earth, first birthed an equal, Uranus, who we know as the starry heavens. Then Gaia bedded Uranus and gave birth to the Titans: Oceanus, Coeus and Crius, Hyperion and Iapetus, Theia and Rhea, Themis and Mnemosyne, Phoebe and Tethys, and the last child, Kronos, who loathed his lusty father. For as soon as each was born, their father Uranus, who hated all, stuffed them back into their mother's body. One by one, he hid them in a cavern of Gaia until she was groaning in pain and anger. Uranus was pleased with his wicked work. Gaia vowed revenge. So out of her own body, she created grey adamant, a metal of fearsome hardness, and fashioned it into a sickle. She showed it to all her dear children, still trapped within her body, and begged one to come forward and help revenge them all for their father's ugly behavior. All were seized by fear except the youngest, Kronos. Gaia placed the sickle in his hand and explained her strategy.

That night when Uranus spread himself over Gaia, lustily stretching out in every direction, Kronos crept out of the body of his mother. Using the weapon she fashioned, Kronos severed his father's genitals and flung them away. Thus ended the suffocation of Gaia, and of her children, who were released from their mother's body.

Scholars conjecture that the sickle used by Kronos became associated with time through a linguistic anomaly: Kronos, a god of agriculture, is mistaken for Chronos, the Greek god of time. The two are conflated in the figure of the Grim Reaper, a god of time and death who appears when our allotted time on earth is up. It is the Grim Reaper who harvests our soul. A linguistic vestige of this idea is the metaphor for untimely death, when we say someone has been "cut down" in the middle of life. We also see visual reminders of this association in modern horror films and in the death card in the Tarot, in which death is personified as a skeleton wielding a scythe.

The crescent moon and the scythe occur frequently in myth, not only in Hesiod's account of creation. The parallels between Gaia's sickle and Psyche's knife proved to be particularly uncanny. The first weapon ever created in Greek cosmology is forged by Gaia, who the Greeks imagine as female, out of her own body. The weapon Gaia creates is shaped like the crescent moon, which is linked to female lunar deities, female reproductive organs (the shape of ovaries and fallopian tubes joining the uterus form a crescent), and the female menstrual cycle. And Gaia forges the sickle to confront an oppressive, suffocating lover. In the story, Uranus stuffs his own children back into their mother's body in a crude and tyrannical attempt to obstruct creation. Without Gaia's protest, and the assistance of her son Kronos in castrating the tyrant, cosmogony would have ceased and we would not have a recognizable, whole cosmos teeming with many forms of life. Without Psyche's willingness to confront Eros, the lovers' paradise would have endured, superficially perfect, perhaps, but not whole or full of life. Psyche's creative instinct, which we see in her urge to create herself, would have been forced to seek other ways to express itself or quietly died from suffocation.

The use of a sharp blade in both stories also brings our attention to the force of emotion that motivated Gaia and Psyche to act. In the depths of Gaia, rage and resentment were stirring. Perhaps similar emotions were also stirring in the depths of Psyche, though in a more disguised manner. I imagine that each one had simply had enough. This is quite clear in Hesiod's account of the strained relations between Uranus and Gaia. But is it really present in "Eros and Psyche"? Perhaps, if we look carefully.

For example, despite Psyche's so-called perfect world, she is lonely and longs to see her sisters. She cannot ignore this longing; like any hunger it grows more acute. When Psyche's sisters arrive, their envy, greed, and spitefulness turn up the fire in an already heated situation. The situation culminates in Psyche's conflicting emotions on the eve of the confrontation. "She delayed. She hurried. She dared. She feared. She despaired. She raged" (Wolkstein 1991, 129). Psyche feels guilt and shame about never having seen her lover; she also fears the truth of the oracle. Apollo had declared that Psyche was fated to marry a monster. Could this be true? The fears for her own life are compounded by fear for the life of her child, a fact Psyche's sisters play upon very effectively. In an emotionally manipulative appeal they tell her that the monster is "indulging you, fattening you, until the time is ripe and your womb is full; then he will devour both you and the child" (127). The sisters' warning is a clever mixture of fact and fantasy, and even a less naïve person than Psyche might be persuaded. Fearful, guilty, despairing, and uncertain—but finally made bold by circumstance—Psyche eventually chooses to confront her lover.

The force of the lunar knife embodies the will of the archetypal feminine in its "drive to consciousness" (Labouvie-Vief 1994, 164). This may help explain why a blade known as a moon weapon symbolizes "the rising power of the feminine" pointing to "the force of the moon, the force of the psychic tides of life, of emotion rather than rational functioning" (Whitmont 1982, 2). Emotions represent energy we cannot, and should not, ignore. For instance, in "Eros and Psyche," the rising power of the feminine appears in the sisters' intuition that there is something monstrous about Psyche's marriage to Eros. They're right. Perhaps Psyche's desire to see her sisters is another intuition, that she needs a different perspective, someone else to see her, and to help her to see. Right again. In the end, we may think Psyche's sisters are despicable, but they are essential. We may rage at Eros's cruelty, but he had to leave.

Long, close experience with the lunar tide of emotion can teach us that emotion has its own intelligence and that we would be wise to pay attention to it. Emotion is the *via regia* between unconsciousness and consciousness. The downward moving impulse, the direction of soul or psyche, honors "the spirit in the hidden meaning of concrete happenings"; when we "go down deep into personal events and into the dark, unknown places of our own emotions" it is there that "we find abundance of life in an intensity of our inward responses" (Ulanov 1971, 183). Or as Jung put it, "emotion is the chief source of consciousness. There is no change from darkness to light or from inertia to movement without emotion" (1954c, par. 179). Yet even today our culture fears deep feeling and emotional expression, one form that repression of archetypal femininity takes. We're encouraged to manage our emotions intelligently rather than acknowledge an emotion's native intelligence. Moreover, we prize control in nearly every aspect of life—resisting the idea that the heat of unruly emotion creates consciousness, willed or no, welcome or not—until we learn to trust our felt sense of things.[43]

A friend of mine, Allison, learned to trust the native intelligence of "an odd little fear," as she thought of it. A few years ago, she mentioned in passing that she'd developed this weird aversion to the long hallway leading to the back of the house. She tried to figure it out, but the only memory she recalled was that of the twisting pathways through the elaborate haunted house her church group constructed at Halloween. While the other kids screamed in delight, Allison had felt real terror. But now it was happening in her home. "It's just a stupid fear," Allison told me. I didn't think so.

The dread didn't go away. In fact, it got worse. Allison could mostly pretend everything was okay when her husband Drew and the kids were home, but even then she began asking them to get something for her rather than retrieving it herself if it required walking down that hallway. "Really stupid," she insisted. I still didn't think so.

Then the dreams began. At first Allison didn't think they had anything to do with the hallway because the images didn't match. There was no hallway in her dream, only something creeping like the thick ground fog that settles in California's Central Valley in winter. Tule fog, the locals call it. In her dream, the fog was alive and menacing. It kept moving slowly toward her. Once or twice she woke up screaming, scaring her perplexed husband. He was the one who encouraged her to get some help, and so Allison started exploring the dream with a movement therapist—unusual, she supposed, but the idea intrigued her. One day when she was enacting the dream, she realized that the stark, cold dread of the menacing fog was exactly like her dread of the long hallway. As it turns out, the feeling wasn't silly at all. As Allison learned to listen, the dread began to speak to her of her forgotten dream of becoming a professional artist. Within a year, Allison began to paint. At first she kept her canvases, paints, and brushes in an unused corner of the living room. One day, her husband said, "Honey, why don't we clean out that back bedroom. Set up a studio for you there?" And so they walked down the hallway together and cleared out the back room. And the dreams of the fog stopped.

Allison's story shows how the rising power of the feminine is the strength to stand up for our own experience as important, not silly, especially when our emotions bring us into conflict with unquestioned values or expectations—what we're supposed to do, or be, or believe, or say. We may have sisters like Psyche's or friends with mixed motivations and their own self-serving agendas at the core of any counsel they offer. Yet even help in this form, with its potential or actual cruelty, can serve us. For instance, we might begin by translating the heavy-handed literalism of such an accusation—"he's devouring you!"—into the possible metaphoric truth it conceals. Turn this into a question and ask, How am I being devoured? or How am I living in a prison? or How am I kept in the dark? We may not like the answers, especially when they stir doubt, confusion, and anxiety. It takes a strong, supple, and resilient person to tolerate the rising power of the feminine and provide a home for unruly and chaotic emotional energies. It makes a person strong, supple, and resilient to do so.

Artemis, Virgin Goddess of the Wilderness

The discovery of Psyche's knife as a lunar weapon associated to the crescent-shaped scythe brings us to Artemis. In the Greek tradition, Artemis is the fiercely autonomous virgin goddess of the wilderness, the hunt, and childbirth. Her early connection to the moon may come from her designation as Phosphoros, or Light-bearer (Otto 1954, 85). She was the "goddess who roves by night," emitting a "brilliant blaze of light" as she hunted (Baring and Cashford 1991, 328). At home in the wild, Artemis has the "rare quality of wildness and its eerie fascination," which we're most susceptible to at nighttime, "when mysterious lights flare up and dart about or the moonlight works magic transformation on field and forest" (Otto 1954, 85). A fine cinematic example of this comes to mind: Harry Potter's Patronus charm, designed to protect loved ones. With a flick of his wand, a brilliant flare of light takes the shape of Harry's animal ally, a wild stag. It takes great skill to produce a fully formed Patronus, and Harry is the first among his classmates to accomplish this feat. Even his adult mentors are surprised at the vivid and powerful creature that comes to life, but I imagine Artemis would be delighted.

The Homeric hymns to Artemis speak of her preference for shadows and darkness. The following passage is one of my favorites:

> She loves to hunt in the shadows of mountains
> and in the wind on mountain-tops
> she loves to take her bow, her solid gold bow,
> stretch it, and shoot off groaning arrows.
> The peaks of great mountains tremble.
> The forest in its darkness screams
> with the clamor of animals,
> and it's frightening. (Boer 1970, 8)

Artemis is particularly associated with one phase of the moon's cycles, the new or crescent moon, because she was a virgin. This links Artemis to "another lunar goddess, the terrible Hecate who personified the dark of the moon and the death-giving powers of women-sorceresses" (Paris 1986, 121–122). These two fierce goddesses expand the range of native femininities that are available to be claimed by women or by men. This feminine power includes "terrible, mortal, and bloody aspects" (ibid., 122). Artemis, the youthful virgin at home among the wild beasts, and the crone goddess Hecate "share an affinity for bloody sacrifice, and the accusation of cruelty does not disturb them" (ibid.).

It is perhaps easier for contemporary readers to associate blood and sacrifice with the crone and not the maiden Artemis. We are suffused with Christian values, which demonize the wisdom of the crone and dignify the purity of the maiden—even going so far as to worship virgin motherhood. But the foundations of Western culture sink deep into Greek soil, where youth and beauty, though exalted, were not always equated with innocence or tenderness. We can see this in the lithe and youthful Artemis who, of all the Greek gods, demanded the bloodiest sacrifices. As the archetypal hunter and therefore a killer, Artemis is "she who slays" (Otto 1954, 84). The remorselessness of this goddess is dramatized in the story of Actaeon. One day, while Actaeon was hunting in the wild with his pack of dogs, he stumbled into an open area where he discovered Artemis bathing. Rather than turn away, he continued to watch the goddess in a clear and offensive act of impiety. When Artemis discovered Actaeon, she did not kill him outright as she so easily could have. Instead, she transformed him into a stag while preserving his human awareness. When Actaeon's hunting dogs caught his scent and turned on him, he was fully conscious about what was happening and knew the inevitable outcome: the living agony of dismemberment. Actaeon's own animals, his companions, tore him to pieces.

There is another way in which the shadowy presence of Artemis in the tale enriches our understanding of Psyche's journey and journeys of the psyche. "Artemis herself is the wilderness, the wild and untamed, and not simply its mistress," says Christine Downing. "Though we may first know her as the other without, she is more truly the other within" (1981, 165). When Psyche confronts Eros in the dark bedroom, she is not only facing Eros as an other for the first time, she is also facing the quality of otherness that exists within her. In this moment, that otherness is characterized by key qualities of Artemis: stealth, alertness, and the willingness to slay.

Whereas Artemis slays Actaeon without remorse, Psyche's situation is far more complex and draws forth a more complex emotional response. Although Psyche may be alert and stealthy, she is not Artemis. She's a mortal girl in love and so she is ambivalent, terrified to confront her mysterious lover who may well be the prophesied monster, and terrified of the consequences of not confronting him. Once she does, she recoils in horror at the idea of nearly killing the beautiful god of love. I imagine that Psyche's horror is partly due to the chasm she has opened between herself and her beloved. Although she has not killed Eros, she has killed their so-called marriage, and her future without him seems like a living death. She has not yet discovered the fullness of Artemis's world.

Psyche's Solitude as Artemisian Space

The distance Psyche creates between herself and Eros is archetypally Artemisian, created by a lunar knife. Lovers will recognize the feel of such a moment, whether the presence of Artemis marks a short hiatus or a final divorce, both of which imply physical separation and perhaps emotional, spiritual, and imaginative distance. Artemis is also present, however, when the separation is not physical at all, for instance, when we feel an emotional or spiritual withdrawal from the other who is right there next to us. It is the advent of a palpable solitude within intimacy that few people relish because, compared to the warmth of erotic passion and tenderness, a move into Artemisian aloneness can feel stark and chilly.

But if movement is life, then the natural oscillation between nearness and distance simply is. Erotic intimacy leads to solitary distance as its archetypal counterpart. Part of the challenge of loving is recognizing that the nearness and the distance are equally authentic. This idea is poetically rendered by Rainer Maria Rilke, who describes the challenge of loving in language that honors Artemisian solitude:

For one human being to love another: that is perhaps
the most difficult of all our tasks, the ultimate, the last
test and proof, the work for which all other work is but
preparation . . . Loving for a long while ahead and far on
into life is—solitude, intensified and deepened loneliness for him who loves. Love is at first not anything that
means merging, giving over, and uniting with another.
(Rilke 1975, 31)

Rilke concludes this passage by asking the essential question,
one that has probably occurred to anyone contemplating the difficulties of true marriage: What would a union be of something
unclarified and unfinished, still subordinate? We can let Eros and
Psyche answer. A union of something unclarified, unfinished,
in which one partner is subordinate to the other would not be
genuine. The alchemists refer to such an unstable union as the
lesser *coniunctio*, an attempt to combine elements that have not
yet been perfectly separated. A lesser *coniunctio*, like the first so-
called marriage of Psyche and Eros, must dissolve because each
lover is not separate enough, not distinct enough. This is one
of the great paradoxes of marriage, captured in the alchemical
maxim, "only that which is separated can unite," an idea Rilke
understood. Dissolution makes way for a different and higher
union, whether that union is with a person or with the self, the
soul, the divine, or something that draws us into a more complete
and whole symbolic marriage.

Psyche's own story offers us two examples of the greater union
that is possible for any of us on a soul journey. The sacred union
with Eros at the end of the tale alerts us to the idea of love as the
eternal partner of the soul. Before that, however, Psyche's lunar
knife gives us another answer. What helps Psyche become psyche
is Artemisian solitude, the place where human companionship
does not serve; Nature itself is ally. I think this insight is particularly important for women to hear because we are culturally
conditioned and perhaps biologically disposed to value caring for
others above ourselves. A retreat into solitude is considered aber-
rant, and few women I know can do it without a sense of guilt.

Historically, few women have been economically, socially, or
politically capable of honoring the Artemisian impulse, nor have

they felt empowered to. Women writers and artists in recent history, those who could afford to nourish the creative instinct apart from necessary work, frequently talk about the need for solitude. The classic and well-known example is Virginia Woolf's 1929 book *A Room of One's Own*. The text is based on lectures Woolf was asked to deliver on the subject of women and fiction the year before. The particular theme she developed was not what women write about, but what they need to create anything at all. As such, *A Room of One's Own* became a sociopolitical indictment of the ways in which women's creative talents are either actively suppressed or never nurtured. Woolf describes Florence Nightingale's "vehement complaint" that "women never have even half an hour that they can call their own" (Woolf 1929, 66). We always are being interrupted. For most women throughout most of history, "to have a room of her own, let a lone a quiet room or a sound-proof room was out of the question" (52).

I can readily appreciate Woolf's point. In my twenties and thirties, I didn't have to carve out a room of my own because I lived alone in apartments. When I married, much later in life than most women, at age 47, I wasn't prepared for the ways in which the atmosphere of a home absorbs and reflects the emotional lives of all the family members. My space suddenly felt very crowded. Because I cherish my creative time and need thick silence to read and write, I devised a simple and elegant solution that was also relatively easy to implement because I'm naturally an early riser: I created energetic space by awakening around four o'clock every morning when my surroundings are dark, fertile, and quiet. This is my ritual, my daily appointment with my soul on behalf of my work.

Dedicating the early morning to my creative work had some unintended benefits for my family. Paradoxically, the more available I was for my solitary creative life, the better I was at creating a home. My solitary hours are not empty at all, nor are they lonely. They are delightfully crowded with figures from a lifetime of dreams and active imagination, figures who move, speak, inspire, admonish, and laugh (yes, at me). These archetypal allies are the rich imaginal gifts of a life centered in the living psyche. May Sarton, another writer who clearly needed solitude, also perceived how honoring Artemis helped her appreciate the power of Aphrodite. "This is what is strange—that friends, even passionate love, are not my real life unless there is time alone in which to explore and to discover what is happening or what has happened," Sarton writes. "Without the interruptions, nourishing and maddening, this life would become arid. Yet I taste it fully only when I am alone here" (quoted in Downing 1981, 168).

Anthony Storr makes an observation similar to May Sarton's. "The capacity to be alone," he argues, is "linked with self-discovery and self-realization; with becoming aware of one's deepest needs, feelings, and impulses" (Storr 1988, 20–21). This is particularly true for individuals who have learned to be compliant. For them, the demands of Aphrodite are oppressive because all human relationship is accommodation. Artemis is an antidote. In her realm, no emotion need be repressed to accommodate another, perhaps contradictory, emotion or to accommodate another person who expects you to behave in a certain way. In Artemisian solitude, where "the very taming of feeling is beside the point," we also can throw off constricting self-expectations from our various social roles (Downing 1981, 172). The freedom can be simultaneously exciting and frightening. I believe Artemis would welcome both emotions.

My favorite literary example of a purpose-built Artemisian refuge comes from the novel *Bleak House* by Charles Dickens, ironically written in an era that celebrated the triumph of man over nature and reason over emotion (Dickens was an intensely ironic author). In that story, John Jarndyce is a generous and loving man who adopts three young people to provide them a safe home, a sanctuary from a world that is cruel and litigious. Jarndyce has the capacity to be gentle, kind, and even-tempered in large part because he has created a sanctuary within his own home where he retreats when "the wind is blowing from the East"—a sign of his impending moodiness and irritability. This room, dubbed "the Growlery," serves exactly as its name implies: it is a place where growling and any other form of bitterness, irritation, rage, and general crankiness are allowed, received, and contained. It is clear from Dickens's novel that without the Growlery, John Jarndyce would be a much less loving and wise man, unable to provide a sanctuary for Esther, Ada, and Richard.

If each of us had our own Growlery, a place of retreat, I believe we would live a richer emotional life. Instead, many of us are like Psyche in the early part of her story, trapped in a luxurious prison, molding ourselves to another's rhythms. Perhaps one of the unexpected gifts of the lovers' separation was that Psyche discovered the purity and uncompromising autonomy of Artemis's realm. Perhaps by fully encountering what was different, wild, and untamed in the vast wilderness, Psyche could begin to understand herself more.[44]

Beloved Nature and Nature as the Beloved

After Eros abandons Psyche, she enters what cultural anthropologists describe as the liminal stage of an initiation journey. The liminal stage, "betwixt and between" two worlds, is brought about by *separatio* and is an experience of *separatio* (Mahdi, Foster, and Little 1987, 5). But such nice, neat concepts have no relevance to the initiate, the suffering human being undergoing the ordeal. For Psyche, it's simply agony. Thinking about what to do or who can help is impossible because it involves thinking—which is impossible. In my own moments of such despair, I know that the world still exists but I just don't care. Allies exist, perhaps. Enemies exist, certainly. But neither matters. When I have the will to notice the purposeful activity around me—noise, movement, light, life—it simply looks very odd and distant, as though I am peering into an alien world.

I imagine Psyche feels just this way: helpless with fatigue and heedless of life. As unwelcome as listless depression may be for an active, decisive, passionate ego, it also may be a refuge for the soul. It is an Artemisian refuge, entirely different from the palatial refuge Eros provides Psyche, yet it is equally essential to the soul's journey, which always has been characterized by a special relationship to gravity, depth, and death.

> Depression is essential to the tragic sense of life. It moistens the dry soul and dries the wet. It brings refuge, limitation, focus, gravity, weight, and humble powerlessness. It reminds of death. The true revolution begins in the individual who can be true to his or her depression. Neither jerking oneself out of it, caught in

97

cycles of hope and despair, nor suffering it through till
it turns, nor theologizing it—but discovering the consciousness and depths it wants. So begins the revolution
on behalf of soul. (Hillman 1975, 98–99)

Because Psyche is true to her depression, we see the revolution
on behalf of soul begin as she accepts the opportune help of nature itself.

The first spirit Psyche encounters is Pan, who urges her to seek
Eros. Psyche heeds his advice and eventually propitiates an enraged Aphrodite, who is seeking Psyche at the same time Psyche
seeks her. The grandiose fury of this goddess makes Psyche appear that much smaller, more vulnerable, and solitary. No wonder she feels despair. Once Psyche begins the series of impossible
tasks assigned by Aphrodite, the spirit of nature in many forms
addresses her, including the ants who help her sort the pile of
seeds, the reed who tells her how to gather the rams' fleece, and
the eagle, who collects the cup of water. In an ordeal in which an
enraged goddess of love opposes her, nature is Psyche's chief ally.
A cynic might say that Psyche had no other choice, but that is the
point. Artemis is present as archetypal midwife, presiding over
the symbolic death and rebirth of the soul, and she is present as
goddess of the wilderness, who symbolizes the vitality of sacred
nature.

It is a paradox that Artemis is a strong presence throughout the
tale while Psyche is most in thrall to Aphrodite. Aphrodite, the
hetaera who relishes erotic entanglement, is present in moments
of blissful union. Artemis, the untamed and inviolable Amazon,
is present in moments of solitude—or what appears to be solitude. Artemis is only a goddess of solitude when seen from the
perspective of Aphrodite. Artemis is more truly an archetype of
a different kind of companionship and not a goddess of abject
loneliness, a truth captured by David Whyte: "To feel abandoned
is to deny / the intimacy of your surroundings" (2009, 77–78).
And though Artemis rejects marriage and male lovers, in classical
poetry she is sometimes described as running, playing, and dancing with her coterie of nymphs. She is "the immanent presence
of the whole of nature as a sacred reality . . . and the living soul
of nature that clothes itself in maiden form, dancing and singing

as the murmuring voices of streams, the rustling of breezes and whispering flowers" (Baring & Cashford 1991, 322). For Artemis, and in Artemis's realm, the wilderness is fresh and alive and surging with the kind of exuberant wildness the goddess relishes. Here is abundance, not scarcity, and many voices, not silence. Artemis guides Psyche to "enter into a living relation with the expressive character of things," a relationship that is reciprocal and as rich as intimacy with humans (Abram 1996, 130). Who better to accompany Psyche in the solitary moments that are a wilderness to a loving, young woman bereft of the one person she has loved and lost?[45]

Artemis, Midwife to the Feminine Soul

When Artemis was nine days old, she helped midwife her twin brother Apollo into the world. Thus the Greeks associated Artemis with the event of childbirth as well as considering her the patron of midwives, mothers, and their young. Childbirth is dangerous, markedly so until very recently. Throughout human history pregnancy has offered the hope of new life and the very real probability of death. As late as the nineteenth century, nearly 50 percent of women died in childbirth. Artemis, a complex goddess who protects the innocent and also hunts and kills, is an apt presence in Psyche's life because she presides over two births in "Eros and Psyche," one literal and one symbolic. The literal pregnancy is the child Psyche carries throughout her ordeal, who ultimately will be born among the gods after the sacred marriage. The symbolic pregnancy is the making of the soul. Artemis, the archetypal midwife, is present to guide the soul's formation.

Of the two, the symbolic child has the weightier presence in the story. Although Psyche is pregnant throughout the four tasks, readers tend to forget this because the child isn't mentioned again until her birth. Or perhaps we don't recall it because the story directs our attention to the making of Psyche, who is also "with child" symbolically, nurturing the seeds of her whole self. Psyche, in this sense, is pregnant with her own future. In describing the symbolic child as it appears in myth from around the world, Jung noted the child's strength as well as its vulnerability in the following passage.[46]

99

The child is endowed with superior powers and, despite all dangers, will unexpectedly pull through. The child is born out of the womb of the unconscious, begotten out of the depths of human nature, or rather out of living Nature herself. It is a personification of vital forces quite outside the limited range of our conscious mind, a personification of ways and possibilities of which our one-sided conscious mind knows nothing—a wholeness which embraces the very depths of Nature. It represents the strongest, the most ineluctable urge in every being, namely, the urge to realize itself. The child is, as it were, an incarnation of *the inability to do otherwise*, equipped with all the powers of nature and instinct (Jung 1954a, par. 289).

For Jung, the divine child personifies vitality because "only the indefinite, fresh, and vital, but vulnerable and insecure, original condition symbolized by the child is open to development and hence is alive" (Edinger 1985, 11). A vulnerable flesh-and-blood infant who is also vibrantly alive reminds us of our own vulnerability as we continually relinquish any belief in mastery to make space for the unknown, the strange, and the other.

An image of fresh, vital, and vulnerable life struck me one day while I was hiking on Mount Tamalpais—for many years my second home, sanctuary, and inspiration. It was a beautiful clear day in April, and the afternoon air was pungent with the aroma of hot pine. This is a smell from my childhood, when I used to run up and down the Oakland hills in the long, spring afternoons after school, playing army with the neighbor kids in the safe jungles of our backyards. As I moved along the trail, I reached out playfully to caress the short, fat evergreen trees on either side of me and was momentarily taken aback by the softness of the lime green needles at the very tips of the branches. This new growth, the vulnerable perimeter of a growing tree that would one day rise more than a hundred feet tall, responded to my touch like feathery blades of tender grass. They were pliable and buttery, irresistibly alive.

Later, while writing in my journal, I reflected that we frail humans are like the small tree, the living potential of some fuller form. Every day we have the opportunity to outgrow ourselves and reach for something beyond our customary identity. It is this new growth that marks the seasons of our lives in the same way that the bright tips of the evergreen marks the return of spring. But that vulnerability is terrifying. Is it even possible to approach the tender places of our own new growth with delicacy and respect? If we did, would we more thoroughly tend the dream of our own becoming?

This exploration of the child archetype—whether imagined as bright tips of an evergreen tree or a newborn infant—raises an intriguing question. How is it that almost no one has questioned the conventional view of Psyche as naïve, simple, tenderhearted, and youthful—in a word, childlike? How is it that even characters within the story insist on viewing her in this one-sided way? Recall, it is Eros and the sisters who persuade us that Psyche is simple, precisely the people who ought to know better. Only a very few readers have seen more deeply into her character. The best assessment comes from Erich Neumann. "This childlike girl, this 'simple and gentle soul' (a masculine misunderstanding if ever there was one!), approaches the sleeper with knife and lamp to slay him. Inevitably her willingness to lose him must burn and wound the masculine Eros most painfully" (1956, 81). Neumann's voice has been overwhelmed by virtually every other interpretation. We simply cannot seem to shake this innocent image of Psyche even though her actions are far from innocent. Psyche not only pulls a knife on her beloved, she indirectly entices her sisters to their deaths.

I suspect that it is the strength of the divine child archetype in Psyche that grips our imagination. We will not let the innocent, vulnerable Psyche go because this is who many of us become when the promise of love appears—no matter how experienced, bitter, wise, conscious, or skeptical we may be. In this moment we are Psyche, the tender-hearted. No matter what we think we know or have learned in other relationships, this love, this time, will make us vulnerable again. The image of the child answers our deep need for a vulnerable soul and a soul journey that compels the attention and assistance of a multitude of powerful allies.

The Agon of Love

From birth through adolescence and into motherhood, Psyche's fate is inextricably intertwined with Aphrodite and Eros. They are the primary deities that shape her life, but she is not inert material in their hands. Psyche contends with them continually, sometimes from afar and sometimes close at hand. It is an agon, a struggle, in which Psyche herself must play a decisive part.

Psyche's story dramatizes the idea that opposition is one way to express devotion. When two people are opposed in the agon of love, the space between them fills with palpable erotic energy that both separates and connects. "Eros and Psyche" teaches us that the psyche is formed within this space, the context of eros, the erotic tension of relationship. A recent example from popular culture illustrates this idea. In the 2009 film *Avatar*, Jake Sully learns Na'vi ways well enough to be given the rare opportunity of participating in the Na'vi initiation rite: choosing, and being chosen by, an Ikran—the powerful flying creature that Jake will bond with for life. As he ventures cautiously forward on the cliff ledge which is crowded with large, agitated, untamed Ikran, he wonders how to choose. Then Jake asks something even more important: "How will I know which Ikran chooses me?" Neytiri bluntly replies, "The one who tries to kill you." This is a fierce test of equality, perhaps most appropriate to someone imagining life as a jungle or a battlefield. Pandora, the setting for the film, is both. Yet it is clear that the ferocity of the Ikran and of Neytiri, who is Jake's beloved, is the other side of their beauty and grace. Facing one another in a fight is a form of mating, the beginning of a deeper bond rather than the end of the relationship. Some may find this repugnant, but I think Psyche and Eros would understand.

We can see this fierceness in our tale: Aphrodite and Eros assist Psyche by opposing her. One of the more beautiful passages in Jung's writing, in which he cherishes opposition, reminds me of Psyche's struggle; it almost could have been written about her: "The soul-spark, the little wisp of divine light . . . never burns more brightly than when it has to struggle against the invading darkness. What would the rain be were it not limned against the lowering cloud?" (1954b, par. 430). Eros wants to keep Psyche in the dark as a possession, preventing a whole relationship characterized by mutual seeing. Aphrodite wants to crush Psyche's every attempt to create an individual, eternal, and sacred union with her lover. Like many of us in such moments, Psyche senses that something is wrong or incomplete or untrue and wants more. She doesn't approach Eros with the intent to kill or destroy—she longs to see and be seen, as fully as possible. That is, Psyche correctly intuits that there may be perfection in wholeness (Jung 1951, par. 123), but there is never wholeness in perfection, as I discussed in chapters 2 and 3.[47] In the end, her rebellion destroys the picture of perfection that Eros's golden palace symbolizes and reveals the underside of love.[48] It is "the beginning of a higher feminine consciousness" (Neumann 1956, 74–75).

Psyche's ability to confront Eros and Aphrodite changes our assumptions about femininity and the feminine soul. By recovering Psyche's knife, we glimpse one who "will discover and express its active, initiating, creative, and transformative capacity" and who will express herself "in the readiness to demand and challenge" (Whitmont 1982, 189). True, this hardly sounds like the simple, naïve Psyche we have come to accept as the character in Apuleius's tale. The story emphasizes Psyche's weariness and despair without attempting to disguise any of it with a show of stalwart invincibility. But it does correspond to the Psyche who sharpens a double-edged knife to confront her lover and the Psyche who survives the withering fury of Aphrodite. As readers, our challenge is to simply watch how, when, and why Psyche is an actor in her own life story yet remains vulnerable, connected to the divinities who shape her life. The vulnerability of the soul makes it permeable to spirit, to the divine. Wounds give us eyes to see, the "errant and renegade" in our behavior is "the God's main route of access" (Hillman 1975, 186). To want an invincible, unwounded Psyche is to denature her. "The psyche would not be loved out of its pathology, nor forgiven. Grace, yes, and caritas, send down what you will, but do not forgive me the means by which the divine powers connect and become real" (ibid.).

Consider the paradox of penetrability. To be penetrable, Psyche must have substance, she must be a substantial being; only then does the influx of the Self hold any meaning at all. This substantial character is formed partly before engagement with the Self and partly through engagement with the Self.[49] It requires both solid strength and radical openness, as Jung makes clear:

> God wants to be born in the flame of man's conscious-
> ness, leaping ever higher. And what if this has no roots
> in the earth? If it is not a house of stone where the fire
> of God can dwell, but a wretched straw hut that flares
> up and vanishes? Could God then be born? One must
> be able to suffer God. That is the supreme task for the
> carrier of ideas. He must be the advocate of the earth.
> (Quoted in Edinger 1985, 115)

Psyche demonstrates her ability to suffer not one but several gods. She is stronger than we have acknowledged, even at the beginning of the story, strong enough to confront Eros with lamp and knife. To borrow Jung's metaphor, she has at least the begin- ning of a house of stone, rooted in the earth. Moreover, Psyche further consolidates her individuality in the struggle with Aph- rodite. It is this Psyche who is so important to us, says Ginette Paris: "Without the trials with which Aphrodite besets her, Psyche would have remained juvenile, not having been measured against any obstacle, and she would not be worth the name she bore, for of what use is a soul that has never known suffering?" (1986, 99). Without Psyche's trials, we would have no story of the soul's relationship to eros and, in fact, no distinctive Psyche worth re- membering at all (Bettelheim 1989, 295).

Aphrodite and Artemis Side by Side

The presence of Artemis, first hinted at through the lunar knife, signifies the plurality of the Self that is guiding Psyche on this path. This lunar goddess of the wilderness and of solitary, vir- ginal autonomy could not be more different from golden Aphro- dite, the sunlit goddess of love and beauty who values intimate relationship above all else. Nor could we imagine truer opposites than Artemis and Eros, though ironically both hunt with a bow and a quiver of arrows. Yet Artemis and Aphrodite are strongly present throughout the myth, their connection most vivid in the moment of conflict. In the same way that the reflected light on

Psyche's knife suggests the moon and hence Artemis, the steady glow of the lamp, which is the primary source of light in the darkened bedchamber, suggests Aphrodite, the golden one. Jung uses a metaphor to describe Psyche's individuation journey that I think both Artemis and Aphrodite would approve of: "The self is our life's goal, for it is the completest expression of that fateful combination we call individuality, *the full flowering . . . of the single individual*" (1928, par. 404; emphasis added). For Aphrodite, this flowering would be shaped and cultivated by human relationship. For Artemis, it would occur within the context of windswept hills, wild grasses, and the profusion of chaotic nature.

What might it mean that these two powerful archetypes, so unalike, are principal guides on the soul's journey? One answer is that Artemis and Aphrodite conjure each other. Aphrodite's beauty, unlike Apollonian beauty, is fleeting, not lasting. Likewise, intimacy with the beloved is an ephemeral experience. Moments of the most intense erotic merging will separate and dissolve into the opposite, periods of solitude ruled by Artemis. Likewise, a surfeit of Artemisian autonomy engenders the kind of intense desire for the other that can transcend physical separation or stimulate the appetite for physical intimacy. The archetypes appear one after the other, as the soul longs alternately for intimacy and autonomy.

The simultaneous presence of Aphrodite and Artemis, symbolically embodied in Psyche's lamp and knife, challenges us to consider these two powers in the story side by side. Jung states that "the one-after-another is a bearable prelude to the deeper problem of the side-by-side, for this is an incomparably more difficult problem" (Jung 1955–56, par. 206).[50] The original relationship between Eros and Psyche is a lesser *coniunctio* in which the individual elements are not sufficiently purified and separated. The convergence of lamp (Aphrodite) and knife (Artemis) exposes the weaknesses in this *coniunctio* and assists in destroying it. Psyche initiates the destruction by breaking the taboo, and Eros completes the destruction by leaving her as he promised he would. Thereafter, the two are physically separated, though linked through Aphrodite. Eros returns home to nurse his wounded shoulder, and Psyche begins the solitary wandering that eventually takes her to the goddess's doorstep. Although the separation of Eros and Psyche may at first appear to be the triumph of Artemis, the story tells us that Psyche is more deeply in love with Eros than ever before.[51] "Enmity promotes the *coniunctio* just as well, maybe even better, than love does" (Edinger 1994, 48–49). The opposite of love isn't hatred. It's indifference.

I believe Eros also is more deeply in love with Psyche, although the story does not say this in so many words. Instead, the evidence is found in Eros's actions near the end of the tale, when he rescues Psyche from a deathly sleep and dares to marry her openly on Mount Olympus, defying his mother Aphrodite and seeking the blessing of the assembled gods. The lovers' separate journeys, one visible, the other invisible, attest to the idea that "love sets up resonances in the deepest abysses of our being. It is a lightning flash of the eternal within the flow of time" and the most authentic, demanding psychological task there is "because it activates in us new ways of knowing ourselves" (Carotenuto 1987, 10, 17). The solitude that Eros and Psyche suffer is not due simply to the fact that they have lost each other and their life together. They have lost everything because nothing will ever be the same. Their experience sets them apart from others because the very power of love is isolating.

Here we can begin to see the *coniunctio* of the two opposing archetypal powers, Artemis and Aphrodite. It is not just that the bliss of intimacy is ephemeral and flows naturally into solitude. It isn't even that whole love includes a measure of hatred and aggression—a resistance to merging with the beloved. After all, Aphrodite's lover is Ares, the Greek god of war and strife, an archetypal pair reminding us that love and strife is inseparable. Artemis and Aphrodite considered side by side reminds us that the experience of love is, as Rilke said, a heightened kind of solitude for the person who loves (Rilke 1975, 31). In the midst of this solitude we can come to know our feelings about and for the other. The space of Artemisian solitude offers us an opportunity to reflect. The purity of Artemisian solitude, where feelings are ours first and owed to no one else, encourages precision in our feelings for the beloved.[52]

Yet let us remember that without the imagined other there might be a lesser storehouse of feelings to mine. Aphrodite's gold can enrich Artemis's realm. Seeing these two great archetypal opposites side by side reveals the great solitudes that exist within intimacy and the profound intimacies that enrich solitude.

5

PHALLIC KNIFE

The erect phallus represents the appearance of life in all its lustiness.
It signals the resurrection of life, coming back into vitality after
a flaccid period of quiet or even after a failure of vitality.

—THOMAS MOORE, *THE SOUL OF SEX*

*After her sisters leave, Psyche spends the day alone, tortured by the plan
to confront her lover that very night. She knows what to do and her
determination is fixed, but still she feels torn between many different
impulses. How is it possible to loathe the beast but love the husband,
though they are one and the same?*

*When night falls, they partake of the combats of love as always, and
then he falls into a deep sleep, as always. But not Psyche. Although she
is still drained from the ordeal of the long, long day, the harshness of
her fate, the fate that wed her to a monster, gives her strength.*

*With a boldness that belies her sex, Psyche uncovers the lamp and
seizes the knife . . .*

As we near the completion of this exploration of Psyche's knife,
we end where we might have started: knife as phallic object. Ever
since Freud made sexual symbolism explicit and the sublimation
of eros a cornerstone of his analysis of culture, we have equated
knives, daggers, and swords with the phallus. They are long and
stiff, and we grip them firmly with one hand, occasionally with
two hands. And clearly a woman who seizes a knife really wants a
penis. Okay, okay. She doesn't really want a penis; she wants what
penises represent—male privilege and power. Naturally, seizing
a knife is a bid for power or an equally obvious compensation for

a lack of power because, well, if you've already got a penis, you don't need to go get one, right?

This kind of cheap reduction of living image to dead symbol is frankly boring. It eliminates the mystery at the heart of the matter that continues to fascinate humanity for one very simple reason: the fleshy penis, despite our best efforts to control it, has always had a life of its own.

You may be asking, how can she write about penises? She doesn't have one. And if she can't write about penises, how can she talk about substitute penises? As I was seriously mulling over these questions, because they did perplex me, I received the delightful gift of a clear and vivid dream.

It is night. The flames of a huge bonfire billow and sway as gusts of cold air, bringing the freshness of vast spaces, sweep across the high plain. In the orange glow, I recognize him. He has visited my dreams before, ever since I was a young girl pouring over picture books of Native American stories, and yet I don't know him at all. I think of him as Eagle Man, because he possesses the visionary strength of the eagle and an exalted sense of his own masculinity. Now, tonight, as though expressing his name, he wears a full headdress of eagle feathers. As I watch him dance in the glow of the firelight, I realize how much I enjoy his graceful power and his indifference to both his abilities and my admiration of them. He is like a magnificent creature supremely unaware of its allure.

Eagle Man invites me to join him, and so I begin dancing by his side, within the curve of his outstretched arm and underneath the protective canopy of the shining feathers. In the next moment, we turn toward each other to make love, smoothly moving into a sexual embrace without stopping the dance. I feel him deep inside of me, then we part before we reach orgasm. As we pull away, I am left with the strong imprint of his rigid phallus. I can feel and see it energetically: it is large, erect, and glowing bright red.

In the days following the dream I could still feel the energetic phallus inside me, especially when I was tuned into my body, for instance, during yoga or while hiking. It was as though climax was not the point because our dance had been an intimacy of a different and more lasting kind. Eagle Man offered me the phallus, a gift that only the generous and abundant masculine can give. I realized in a very intimate way that the penis and the phallus are two different things. As a female, a penis is not part of my biological endowment, and I cannot begin to speak about the penis in the same way a male would. But the phallus, as Thomas Moore says, "is the penis mythologized," seen in its archetypal rather than biological form, and thus "available to men and women, whether they are waving it in a procession, pleasuring it in sex, or strapping on a rubber one" (1998, 38, 40). As a human being, I can legitimately speak about the phallus.

Making the move from flesh to image is not an easy step. Recognizing the phallus as an archetype equally available to men and women is an embodied insight that stirs emotion, imagination, and intellect and leads to substantive changes in self-perception and behavior.[53] Let's see how.

From Male Penis to Masculine Phallus

The phallus expresses a masculine form of potency that can and does appear spontaneously to any of us, regardless of our sex (male or female, an anatomical distinction) or our gender (masculine or feminine, a cultural distinction).[54] Few people artfully maintain this important distinction. Even intellectual leaders within the field of depth psychology such as Freud and Jung had dogmatic attitudes toward masculine and feminine and have been justly criticized for it.[55] Jung, for instance, attempted a holistic approach by theorizing that our biological sex was counterbalanced by its psychological opposite. A man's inner feminine is his anima, whereas a woman's inner masculine is her animus. So far so good. When we look closely, though, it is apparent that Jung had a much higher opinion of the anima than the animus. Whereas the anima enhances a man's character by adding depth and soulfulness, a woman's animus renders her judgmental, opinionated, and irritating.[56] This may prove Patricia Berry's observation that "dogma in psychology exists frequently where we are most fuzzy, not necessarily where our attitudes are sharp and unyielding" (1982, 43). The sharp tone of dogmatic language acts as compensation for the embarrassment of fuzziness when it is too humiliating to admit to confusion and uncertainty.

Andrew Samuels, among others, offers a way out of the dogma that helps us understand Psyche's knife. Rather than attempting to define what is archetypally masculine based on sexual maleness or what is archetypally feminine based on sexual femaleness, he advocates seeing the sexual body as a metaphor for otherness: "A man will imagine what is 'other' to him in the symbolic form of a woman—a being with another anatomy. A woman will symbolize what is foreign to her in terms of the kind of body she does not herself have. The so-called contrasexuality is more something contra-psychological; anatomy is a metaphor for that" (1989, 103–104). Thus animus and anima are archetypes of an other way of being, thinking, and acting—what is strange to me, different, perhaps a little discomforting, but in all respects "not I." A predominantly feminine person (not necessarily a girl or woman) is likely to imagine that other as masculine, whereas a predominantly masculine person (again, not necessarily a boy or man) is likely to imagine the other as feminine. To be even more precise, anima and animus manifest as what is "not I" and alluring.[57] If a woman is receptive, yielding, or passive in this moment, then the contrapsychological other for her would be assertiveness, drive, and activity. It has less to do with whether someone is a particular sex (male or female) or a particular gender (masculine or feminine) than it does with their expressed character. The element of time is important, too. Human beings are so intellectually and emotionally complex that who we are right now in the immediate present crucially shapes what is other—but again, only right now.

We might expect that it would be easier to distinguish masculinity and femininity as modes of being when observing a male and a female. Not so. Often these archetypal proclivities are more evident between members of the same sex, since we typically expect men and women to be more different than similar. For example, a man's passivity may appear in sharper relief when he is in the company of his assertive younger brother. Or, in "Eros and Psyche," the sisters' aggression starkly contrasts Psyche's indolence. Using the lens of cultural history offers us another way to distinguish the many modes of gender expression. We could, for instance, observe the evolution of images of the feminine over time, contrasting two prominent women in the same role such as Nancy Reagan and Michelle Obama. Both are powerful women in the public eye, married to powerful men, and serving as First Lady. But note how differently they express their femininity and their masculinity.[58] Furthermore, just as it's often more difficult to identify archetypal masculinity and femininity when comparing a man and a woman, it's also difficult when observing a person who has moved closer to psychological androgyny—which is the move toward wholeness. I define such androgyny as the facile and fluid movement among multiple modes of being, including many kinds of masculinities and many kinds of femininities. Like being able to discern the brush techniques of a truly accomplished painter, it requires very close study and a subtle eye for nuance.

Once again, we are making fine distinctions. We are using a razor-sharp blade, if you will, to sort through the meaning and significance of masculine and feminine. Making fine distinctions is the best way to place Psyche's knife clearly as a phallic object in context, which is its role in the moment when Psyche uses the knife against Eros. That context is crucial for understanding her behavior and how archetypal images operate because it is not just any knife we are dealing with, it is Psyche's knife. So the question is not, How is the knife phallic? The question is, How is Psyche's knife phallic? In adopting the keen and discriminating perspective of the knife we are following Jung's lead, treating the knife itself as a mode of apprehension, a way of seeing, or an approach to our subject (for further information, see Jung 1954b; see also Hillman 1975). The sharp knife can help us do the precise work of amplification, to get beneath the dull and leaden stereotypes of knife and of phallus.

Men and Their Penises

To discover what is or is not phallic, let's begin by listening to men describe their penises. The first thing that becomes obvious is that the penis has a life of its own quite separate from the man's will. This is a source of consternation, anxiety, wonder, and embarrassment which sometimes fosters in a man the sense that his entire body is alien. It is "an objective thing from which he differentiates himself, as though it doesn't belong to him," says Helmut Barz, in an honest and poignant scholarly discussion of this topic. "As a boy, I often heard 'his manhood' spoken of, when referring to the genitals of a boy or man. One's manhood, that is to say, is precisely localized and can be grasped in the hand. In addition, it is present from the beginning and makes its independence unmistakably clear early on" (1991, 43). According to Sam Keen, a leader in the men's movement, the penis issue boils down to whether or not this autonomous organ is going to do what it's supposed to do when it's supposed to do it. In sex, the man, not the woman, is "the one who has to get it up at just the right minute and keep it up until everything comes out right" (Keen 1991, 69). Performance anxiety is a painful reminder that the penis has a mind and a will of its own, connected to the male but somehow disconnected from him, too.

The penis seems to epitomize autonomy, which may be why it was depicted in Greek and Roman art with wings and legs. Catherine Johns, a scholar of Greek and Roman erotic imagery, points out that transforming the penis into "a small independent animal may stress the independent nature of the organ, often very much less under its owner's control than he might wish" (1989, 68). Winged and legged penises in Greco-Roman art may strike the modern eye as amusing, peculiar, or even repugnant. But the autonomy of the penis is not an anachronistic idea, belonging to another age without relevance to contemporary culture. There is a clear basis in the male experience for the penis as a separate, independent, and ultimately uncontrollable organ. Simply, it is obvious whether the penis is erect or not, and it is equally obvious that this in not something entirely within a man's control.

A man's ability to grasp his penis and, by analogy, to "get a grip on himself," probably inspires at least two of the slang terms that are used for the penis, *tool* and *weapon*. It is also a reason that a knife, which is both a tool and a weapon, is considered phallic. A man's identity, his very sense of himself as a person, is oriented around his phallic sexuality. *Manhood* is a metaphor for *penis*, but it is a synecdoche for *male:* the part (penis) stands for the whole (person). The man himself is an object that can and ought to be manipulated or controlled just like his tool, or any tool. The idea that the penis fundamentally stands for maleness partly explains the emphasis on erection and size. "Size does matter," a phrase that appeared in contemporary American pop culture a few years ago to advertize the film *The Hulk*, is not a new claim. The importance of size has been prevalent across cultures and throughout history. Glance through any collection of erotica from around the world and you will see "erection after erection, towering, triumphant" (Keen 1991, 70). To explain this emphasis on exaggerated size and stiffness, Keen candidly offers two very different interpretations:

> The quick and easy answer is that men are horny to
> the core and naturally celebrate the phallus in its proud
> stance. Larger-than-life erections are monuments to
> exuberant masculinity. Sure enough, every man knows
> those moments when his cock rises, stands tall, and is
> so full of the primal mystery that it seems a natural
> object of worship. It has an awesome life of its own
> and is deserving of hymns of praise. . . . The slow and
> difficult answer is that our focus on erection is also
> a compensation for our feelings that the penis, and
> therefore the self, is small, unreliable, and shamefully
> out of control." (70)

What we see in Keen's description is that the penis isn't just a penis—and it isn't just a symbol of his phallic sexuality or power. It is a symbol of his very character, himself. A towering, triumphant cock symbolizes a towering, triumphant man.

Freud, the Penis, and the Phallus

Why differentiate the penis from the phallus at all? In part, it is a necessary response to Freud. The father of psychoanalysis believed that human beings were naturally bisexual and that the notion of gender difference was based on a child's first glimpse of the penis. Freud then outlined four stages of normal childhood development that revolved around the recognition and acceptance of sexual difference. Developing a healthy relationship to the penis was critical for both little boys and little girls, but each sex had to contend with sexual wounding. For boys, it was the fear of losing the penis, or castration anxiety. For girls, it was longing to have the penis, or penis envy. In either case, it is the fear of not being whole.

Although it is tempting to read Freud literally, to do so would be to read him badly. In a conversation with Christine Downing, she pointed out that Freud has a predilection for bodily metaphor and frequently uses the rhetorical device of synecdoche, which is taking the part for the whole. Penis is not the literal penis, but a symbol for the power and autonomy that males are accorded in Western culture—privileges that they continually fear that they will lose and that females justifiably envy. The result, Downing says, is that castration anxiety and penis envy become ways of talking about some of the most fundamental concerns associated with our gendered existence. Downing believes that Freud's language demonstrates a compassion for our common woundedness rather than any moral judgment: "To speak of the soul or the body is always to speak of suffering" (personal conversation, November 2000).[59]

One form our common human suffering takes is in wanting what we don't have. For instance, the desire for phallus can too easily be judged as envy or perversion. It's all fine and good for a woman to sexually desire her lover's phallus, but if women want their own phalluses and there is confusion between the male penis and the archetypal phallus, the situation is likely to be misconstrued. A woman becomes an envious female, eternally frustrated because she doesn't and can't have a penis and therefore doesn't and can't have a phallus. Or worse, the desire for the phallus is taken to mean a woman is an envious castrating female, depriving a male of his penis because he has what she wants. Each alternative presupposes a zero-sum game, in which one person wins only when the other loses. But the archetypal world doesn't operate according to zero-sum rules. The sacred phallus is abundantly and equally available to men and women. It "represents life's potency in the largest sense, something we all need and crave," says Thomas Moore. "There is nothing neurotic or egotistical about desiring the fertility and potency that are epitomized and compacted into this image" (1998, 39).

One of my students, who had been creating phallic sculptures for years, chose to explore the relationship between women and the phallus in her doctoral research. Anne Gustafson worked with the phallic sculptures of artist Louise Bourgeois, recording her personal associations to the images, cultural associations to the phallus in myth and history, and finally creating works of art in response to each Bourgeois sculpture she studied. It is a deeply creative and meaningful work, whose power to shape her life surprised her. In the conclusion to her work she writes:

> This experience of the phallic as a living energy that exists within my own body not as a male reproductive organ but more in the location of my backbone, keeping me upright and offering internal stability, was shocking and empowering. . . . Inquiring into this image was like getting an injection of living, breathing self-confidence. Perhaps that is why I started riding motorcycles around the same time; perhaps I need to act out physically the experience of a burst of rushing energy, the speed and confidence of handling a large, fast machine being an expression of my newfound phallic energy! . . . [At the same time] I became aware that by definition the phallic form indicates the presence of the feminine, because one defines the other. Without the solid, defining presence of the phallic, the surrounding feminine is too formless; without the surrounding, containing feminine, the phallic is unimaginable. (2011, 257)

Gustafson's research shows clearly that the phallus is an archetype abundantly available to each of us. Moreover, the appearance of the masculine phallus in her dreams, her artwork, her new interests, and in a new sense of core vitality and strength did not obliterate the feminine. On the contrary, it helped define it.

One could argue that a woman's desire for phallic power is an implicit acknowledgment that female or feminine power is inadequate, incomplete, or inferior. Look closer, and once again we see zero-sum rules in operation, archetypal penury in which every gain must be offset by an equivalent loss. According to this logic, the reason a woman seeks phallic power is because of what she lacks—or worse, what she disrespects and devalues. Hence, a woman desiring phallic power is somehow betraying the sisterhood, paying homage to the very thing that symbolizes millennia of oppression. There is little question that phallic power, misunderstood and crudely applied, is oppressive. But that says much less about phallus as archetype and far more about those who have embodied it. For Gustafson, the power of the phallus was an internal sense of her own strength and uprightness that manifested in an enhanced ability to stand up for herself and for others who needed her protection. The wise use of phallic power by a woman or a man has grandeur and dignity, as does the wise use of its equivalent—uterine power. They are simply distinctive styles of expressing power.

Jacques Lacan, who explored the meaning of the phallus, reached a simple and profound conclusion: by virtue of its turgidity, the phallus is the image of the vital flow as it is transmitted in generation (2002, 277).[60] Lacan thinks beyond the sexual function of the penis/phallus and speaks of flow and generativity as psychological capacities. This is an important and liberating move. A man contemplating his phallic power might reflect on how his life is exuberant, vital, and creative in many different arenas, the bedroom being only one of them. He might consider his progeny in a symbolic sense—not merely human children but his more-than-human legacy, that which he creates and leaves behind, the fruits of a generative life. What am I giving to the world? he might ask. How will my efforts and energy live on? These kinds of questions are sharpened by the prospect of death, as we reflect and sum up a life. They are part and parcel of the sting of existential angst that affects some people no matter how vibrantly creative they have been. Reframing phallic power as more than sexual power brings to the Freudian conversation a deeper understanding of phallic anxiety. Losing the vital flow and generativity expressed by the phallus, or believing that we cannot and do not legitimately have it, is akin to death.[61]

The phallus is one archetypal image of vital, creative flow, but not the only one. To be sure, the natural exhibitionism of the erect penis guarantees that it is an obvious and unmistakable image for this quality, but exhibitionism serves another purpose. The showy penis evokes the sense of divinity that male authors mention. On this note, Jungian analyst Eugene Monick makes the wry observation that the penis "is wondrous and at the same time very odd as a taskmaster. That is what religious people have always said about gods" (1987, 20). This description recalls how Sam Keen described his cock as "so full of the primal mystery that it seems a natural object of worship. It has an awesome life of its own and is deserving of hymns of praise" (1991, 70). Like the male penis, the archetypal phallus insists on its own presence and demands recognition. It is not very subtle in expressing its desire. On the contrary, it is felt as a sudden, unmistakable surge of energy that may not be repressed or ignored. It is no surprise, then, that the phallus is described as an archetype of potency, thrust, and penetration. It is the flow of vitality that begins from within and surges outward.

Phallus and Connection

Archetypal phallus is not simply a flow of vitality or energy; it is directed toward something specific. This idea is congruent with the male experience of erection. Men describe it as a sudden surge of desire in response to something or someone quite specific; a touch, a look, a scent, an image, the sound of a voice on the phone or someone's laughter across the room. "The erect phallus represents the appearance of life in all its lustiness," says Thomas Moore (1998, 120). This needn't be merely sexual or sensual lust. "At times, a sudden erection totally unrelated to sexual desire will occur," notes Jungian analyst Robert Stein, "which suggests that the phallic rush of energy into the penis is a spirit which transcends the sexual drive" (1998, 97). Arousal can be inspired by a variety of situations and stimuli, for instance, the idea of winning an athletic contest or successfully negotiating a business deal. Someone can even become aroused by the smell of napalm in the morning, to quote a memorable cinematic moment. This variety of lusty inspirations is as surprising as it is delightful. Who knew that life could be such an endless smorgasbord of turn-ons?

Equally surprising, however, is that the archetypal phallus can be seen as a connecting impulse, one that recognizes or creates relationship between itself and the other. This is counter to many of our most cherished images of masculinity which celebrate aloof independence, going it alone, and solitude to the point of loneliness, whereas our cherished images of femininity emphasize intimate relationship. Consider, for a moment, images of father, king, or emperor. At this cultural moment, they tend to evoke a solitariness that images of mother, queen, or empress do not. When a male leader is solitary, he is heroic. When a female leader goes it alone, she's cold, unfeeling, a snob or a bitch. A recent bumper sticker and billboard campaign reminds men that good fathers spend time with their children. Why the reminder, unless we fear that it's necessary?

When Jung attempted to speak archetypally about the essential qualities of masculinity and femininity, he used the terms *eros* and *logos* as "conceptual aids to describe the fact that woman's consciousness is characterized more by the connective quality of Eros than by the discrimination and cognition associated with Logos." Eros is an expression of woman's "true nature," he says, "while their Logos is often only a regrettable accident" (Jung 1951, par. 29). Current social science research into adolescence affirms this difference: young girls moving into womanhood are far more preoccupied with social relationships that express the connective quality of eros than are young boys.[62] In social science terms, women seek connection, men seek solitude. In the language of the archetypal, the feminine connects, the masculine separates. Yet in Greek mythology, Eros is a male god, hence a god with a penis and therefore a specifically phallic figure. A phallic god, by virtue of his maleness interested in separation and not connection, is the driving force behind archetypally feminine connecting consciousness. The quick explanation might be that Eros is about relationship only as long as he dominates. Looking at the myth can prove this very point: the moment Psyche disobeys the god and disrupts their perfect existence—the moment she makes an aggressive and transgressive move—Eros leaves. But there's more to the story, which I'll return to later.

The phallus is often thought of as an aggressive weapon, a tool of power. The relationship it seeks is one of domination. To connect is somehow to obliterate or destroy the other, not to enjoy or meet it. There is no doubt whatsoever that domination is one way that phallus expresses itself. The statistics on rape and sexual abuse of all kinds, directed toward both children and adults, is sobering evidence. The violent imagery in some pornography, reports on the evening news, and horror stories from battlefields around the world are yet more evidence. We are so inundated with such imagery that we can too easily forget that this is only one way that the archetypal phallus expresses itself. (And furthermore, the phallus is not the exclusive archetype of domination, nor are aggression and violence archetypally masculine.)

Domination is one form of connection, however difficult it may be to imagine it as connection at all. In fact, it would more properly be called sadism, a dark form of eros explored by Thomas Moore (1994a). The important point for our discussion is that the surge of vitality and flow of energy characteristic of the archetypal phallus can be domineering, tyrannical, and sadistic, but it can also be a creative or pioneering drive as well. There is a terrific scene in the film *Pollock*, a biography of the abstract expressionist Jackson Pollock, which perfectly expresses this phallic surge as creative initiative. While still a relatively unknown artist, Pollock received a commission that gave him the wide attention that any young artist might crave. He was to paint an enormous canvas for the New York City townhome of Peggy Guggenheim. The work was so large that Pollock had to knock down some of the interior walls of his studio to have room to stretch the canvas and paint it. The scenes of his frenzied activity with a sledgehammer, noisily breaking through lath and plaster, give way to the dramatic unfurling of the canvas, which in turn fade into scenes of nearly absolute stillness, as Pollock hunkers in front of the big, blank expanse for days on end, frozen in place except for the cigarettes he lights, smokes, and tosses away, one after another after another. It seems like agony, and it is an agon, though between who and what isn't entirely clear. Then the camera closes in on Pollock's eyes. They narrow like a predator and then widen, the irises dilated and black in a clear sign of physical arousal. With one powerful lunge, he leaps toward the canvas with his brush and begins painting. From that moment, until the work is finished, there is no stopping him. This is phallic power: Pollock's attempt to connect to the image in his mind's eye and then connect with the canvas.

Robert Stein explains that the phallus moves "towards penetration of an unknown realm," which is a good description of

Pollock's blank canvas (1998, 98). It's an equally apt description of the blank page awaiting the writer, the blank score ready for the composer, the empty studio that holds the choreographer, or the beginning state of any creative endeavor. The phallus is, therefore, "fundamental to human initiative. Without it we can be moved, but we cannot move. Anyone who fears being moved out of old stable structures into areas that are new, unknown, and unformed, will fear the sudden, irrational influx of Phallos" (ibid.). The phallic drive can perhaps best be understood in contrast to the archetypal womb, another image of creativity. The womb, however, is structured to receive, contain, and gestate; it is the moved, not the mover. The womb's drive, if it can be called that, is characterized by stillness and slow growth, quiet, depth, and interiority. By contrast to the showy phallic drive, the womb's aspect of creativity is secret, private—even invisible for a long time and far into the future.

The phallic drive to connect is obvious, not secretive, and focused, not vague. It has a penetrating quality that can be overwhelming or invasive, but isn't necessarily so. This depends partly upon the conscious or unconscious intention behind the phallic thrust and partly upon the response to this thrust. In fact, I think we can say that a large part of how the phallus is perceived is conditioned by how it is received. The particular expression of phallic energy in any given moment depends on both participants, the initiator and the recipient. To understand this with a simple example, consider the various ways someone can greet you with the question, How are you? Imagine different kinds of body language—including posture, gesture, and tone of voice—and how you might react. If you perceive the questioner as aggressive or invasive, you may physically recoil, freeze, or return aggression for aggression. If you perceive the questioner as excited and interested, you may feel a similar surge of eagerness. The style and quality of the relationship matter, underscoring the point that eros is, fundamentally, an archetype of connection.

Eros as a Phallic God

It is now possible to see why Eros, a phallic god and one of the principal deities of the Greek pantheon concerned with fertility and sexual matters, is also the god of love (Johns 1989, 54). This is not only because he is the son of Aphrodite; Eros's role as a connecting force predates his relationship to the Greek goddess of love and beauty. According to the Orphic tradition, Eros "is a maker of worlds. We know that he makes relationships, friendships, families and communities, even nations" (Moore 1992, 150). In the Platonic tradition, eros makes relationships through the force of sexual desire and is an intermediary between the human and the divine. Eros also rules social intercourse that is particularly deep and intimate, a meeting of minds that is nearly sexual in its effect. This is most evident, perhaps, in Plato's *Symposium*, where the men gathered around the table are discussing eros itself (Hamilton & Cairns 1961, 555).

Eros "also inspires poetry, letters, stories, memories and shrines" (Moore 1992, 150). But notice that each of these creative activities is inspired by separation. We write letters to speak to someone who is absent; we write stories and poetry and share memories to preserve or commemorate the past; we build shrines to honor the dead. Eros, the phallic god, rules moments when separation and connection coincide, or when the feeling of separateness inspires the drive to connect. In fact, it would be more accurate to describe eros as an archetype of lack or absence, of wanting what we don't have. The power of eros is most vivid in the absence of the beloved or when we are reaching across a gap that no amount of desire or striving can ever close. This is a point that poet and scholar Anne Carson makes beautifully: "Whoever desires what is not gone? No one. The Greeks were clear on this. They invented eros to express it" (1998, 11).

When we consider the phallic nature of Eros, key moments in the myth come into focus. The first moment is what we might call Eros's failure. Sent by his mother Aphrodite to make Psyche fall in love with a monster, Eros fails in his mission. He falls in love with her instead. If Eros had not fallen in love with Psyche and asserted himself, taking the woman he wanted in a clearly phallic action, we would have no meaningful story of the soul's suffering and no story of the suffering and transformation of Eros. This is a reminder not to label something a failure too quickly. In fact, when listening to another person's story, it is fascinating to note the ways in which failure has had an intentional, meaningful role to play in the individuation process, which is clearly the case with Eros and Psyche. As discussed in chapter 2, although Eros did not literally make Psyche fall in love with a monster, his clandestine relationship with Psyche is in some ways monstrous.

It is also possible to see Eros's action as a volatile and psychologically revealing mix of obedience and disobedience. He clearly doesn't obey Aphrodite's order. His own erotic urge preempts this, a pointed reminder that even the god who is desire incarnate cannot control desire. Next, Eros attempts to cover up his disobedience by spiriting Psyche away to a gorgeous palace, hidden from the eyes and ears of Aphrodite. He spends his nights with Psyche but shows up on Mom's doorstep each morning. At this point in the story, Eros is the obedient *puer*, son-lover of the goddess, childlike and immature. Perhaps this is why Eros sets such rigid rules for his relationship to Psyche and is so outraged when she transgresses them. It may be that his domination of Psyche, an expression of the towering and triumphant phallus (as ego), is an attempt to compensate for submission to his mother, an expression of the pitifully small and weak phallus (as ego).

Eros becomes a fully phallic god only at the end of the tale, the first step being his willingness to go to Psyche and awaken her from the deathly sleep to which she had succumbed in applying Persephone's cosmetic. The next and more important step was Eros's willingness to declare openly and to defend the thrust and intention of his desire, without shame or embarrassment, among the Olympians. By petitioning the greatest of all the phallic gods, Zeus, to sanctify his marriage to Psyche, Eros proves himself to be more than the son-lover of a powerful goddess. He becomes a mature phallic male god in his own right, fully expressing the archetypal power of love and desire. This is the Eros "who is not only powerful, he is also beautiful, full of life and grace" (Moore 1992, 149).

The willingness of Eros finally to bring his marriage to Psyche out from secrecy and darkness demonstrates his phallic brilliance, since phallus, among other things, means light. In this respect, Eros's erection is "not an emblem of blunt power, it is his showing" (ibid.). Ironically, this phallic shining, which Eros could fully achieve only by separation from Aphrodite, makes his connection to Aphrodite more pronounced. The brilliant, phallic Eros shines in a specifically masculine way, in the urge to take possession, to capture, whereas the brilliant golden aura that Aphrodite exudes is a specifically feminine form of allure, "the magic of an appearance that draws irresistibly into the ravishment of union" (Otto 1954, 101). Aphrodite enraptures and Eros captures. Between them, they express two aspects of the erotic that make passion the interesting dance that it is.

The mature Eros who reenters the story near its end truly becomes husband to Psyche and father to a new archetype, their child Pleasure. It is this Eros, not the *puer*, who can provide "the soul's need for all that eros offers, for a world that holds together and a whole life that is creative and motivated by love" (Moore 1998, 13). Although Eros is not as prominent in the myth as Psyche, his character has a clear and compelling arc that dramatizes the full development of phallic power in a male god. By the end of "Eros and Psyche," Eros embodies and integrates both aspects of the phallus. The result is a whole marriage to Psyche.

Erotic Privacy and the Archetypal Womb

Some commentators on the myth believe that Eros's desire for secrecy displays an important aspect of the erotic. Phallic thrust seeks containment in the dark womb. Thomas Moore, for example, states that "eros wants darkness, privacy, secrecy, both in our literal bedrooms and figuratively as part of the intimacy lovers share. Love and the soul flourish in a deeply interior space, free of the ideas and judgments of the world, in a place of their own" (1998, 98). Another Jung scholar who picks up this theme of privacy is John Ryan Haule, who notes that "to know and be known by our beloved, we must be in an important sense alone while we are together" (1992, 204). In chapter 4, "Lunar Knife," we pondered the need for space between lovers in an intimate relationship, noting that paradoxical truth that Aphrodite and Artemis conjure each other; indeed, they exist side by side. What Moore and Haule point out, though, is that a couple must preserve their own solitude and privacy with respect to the world. Psyche and Eros have privacy: no one among their intimates even knows of the relationship, not until Psyche begs and pleads to see her sisters. What they lack is the formally acknowledged container for their marriage that, on the one hand, is tacit permission to enjoy lovers' privacy and the necessary boundary to ensure that they can enjoy it.

The womb is an image of the kind of containment, privacy, and interiority that marriages need. If we assign masculine to male and feminine to female, we would naturally think that a husband seeks containment in his wife. But when we recall the roving homes of masculinity and femininity, it is clear that either partner can offer the beloved the warmth and privacy of the archetypal womb. Jung's essay (1931) on marriage as a psychological relationship makes precisely this point. He speaks about two complementary roles apportioned to the partners. One person is the container and the other is the contained. As illuminating as it is to see these two roles, container and contained, divided between the couple, it still falls short of a full archetypal enactment of healthy relationship. Ideally, both partners learn to be containers for the other and also learn to be contained; the roles are not fixed. Moreover, the womb is an image of the larger container that the couple must create together to contain them both, which allows them the privacy they need together, away from the world, the sanctuary to which they each can turn when they need feminine containment.

What might the marriage womb look like, the container to which the couple can retreat together to tend their relationship? "Eros and Psyche" offers one problematic answer: the luxurious palace the lovers inhabit when Eros first falls in love with Psyche. It is a sensual paradise where every want is satisfied: delicious food, elaborate baths, silken clothing, and lovely music. It truly is a refuge from the world. But Psyche intuits that it is more like a prison and the rules are strict. Moreover, Eros does not truly share it with her in any genuine sense; it is not their home, one they create together as an expression of their love. He simply arrives after dark and leaves before dawn, when it's convenient for him. In fact, the so-called marriage of Psyche and Eros at the beginning of the story shares many of the qualities of a traditional division of power between husband and wife. Hers is the domestic arena (admittedly, with all her domestic chores taken care of) while his arena is the entire world. For Psyche it is too small, too lonely. Some part of her realizes that no matter how perfect it may seem, it is not whole. Paradoxically, her bold action with lamp and knife makes it possible for the lovers to reconstitute their marriage container, except that one key element is missing: the stability of trust and meaning, as Nathan Schwartz-Salant describes:

> Any deep relationship has its elements of heaven and hell; but when it is a process characterized by a stability of trust and meaning, hard won through many trials of betrayal and failure to meet the demands of intimacy, a resilient container is created which better enables each partner to live through the turmoil, tragedies, joys, and difficulties of life. When partners know and experience each other through chaos and destructiveness as well as through beauty and growth, they create a container which encourages and supports the process of individuation and which becomes a person's most sacred possession. (1998, 219)

Contrast the palace of Eros with a different example of a conjugal container from Greek classical culture: the great marriage bed of Odysseus and Penelope. At the end of the *Odyssey*, when Odysseus has returned after twenty long years of warfare and wandering, Penelope doesn't recognize him. In fact, so many suitors have vied for her hand that she is justly suspicious of this newest visitor who claims to be her absent husband. To test him, she asks Odysseus to move their bed. He reacts with surprise and indignation: how could Penelope, of all people, forget that the bed cannot be moved? He himself carved one of its posts from a living olive tree, firmly rooted in the earth beneath their palace. Here, the marriage bed is not merely a lovely container but is itself an organic part of their identity, a secret that Odysseus and Penelope share unbeknownst to the score of suitors hanging about. It cannot be uprooted without destroying something sacred—and that Odysseus is unwilling to do.

Another example, this one from the Jewish tradition, shows how this container can be time rather than a place. The Sabbath, which begins at sundown on Friday evening and ends before sundown on Saturday, divides time. It is a day when Jews turn their attention away from worldly things toward the sacred. This includes the sacred bond of husband and wife. Sex is encouraged throughout the week, but sex on the Sabbath is a mitzvah, an obligation that is also a celebration of the blessing that is life and love.

The feminine container for the couple, whether it is a place in the mind or heart or a home, a room, or the marriage bed, fosters full erotic expression. It welcomes both urges, the masculine urge to penetrate and the feminine urge to receive, expressed by either partner at any given moment. The first so-called marriage of Psyche and Eros lacked this private space, despite the fact that they were sequestered in a palace and spent each night alone together. The darkness that enveloped them was more like a veil between the lovers than a canopy surrounding, embracing, and protecting them. Eros, who insisted on this darkness, used it to maintain distance from Psyche. He failed to understand that the privacy lovers enjoy is a privileged seeing, not the absence of seeing. True lovers explore each other as fully as possible with touch and also with the gaze. "The sexual gaze has strong emotional power and is mysteriously and fundamentally meaningful," notes Thomas Moore, having "something in common with the religious gaze" (1998, 85). This gaze is a kind of rapt attention and a form of rapture. On one level it can be described as blindness—we fail to see past the other's presentation of self; on another critically important level this is sight that penetrates to a depth that otherwise would be invisible. "When I present myself to the gaze of my lover, I am making a gift. I'm letting down my tools of self-protection and my defenses, exposing myself not just to an eye's perusal but to a soul's reflection. I am being seen not just in my physical stature, but in my very being" (108). John Haule, like Thomas Moore, emphasizes the element of trust, pointing out the delight of discovery that only the lover's gaze makes possible:

> I learn to know my beloved down to her minute detail,
> and I see deep into the inner space of her world. . . .
> I see something that perhaps no one else has been
> fortunate to behold. I sometimes may see what she has
> never known about herself; and in my seeing, I reveal
> it to her—just as she discloses new vistas of my inner

space. Our lenses enable us to become explorers of one another's continents and seas; and at the same time we come to know our own. (1992, 20–21)

Allowing ourselves to be thus seen is an expression of profound trust. Eros did not trust Psyche in this way.

The taboo Eros imposed against seeing was a taboo against being seen. By conducting their relationship entirely in the dark, Eros limited the lovers' mutual exploration. He prevented Psyche from knowing him in his very being, with her eyes as well as her body. He was willing to penetrate her sexually, but he was unwilling to be penetrated by Psyche's deep gaze. Of course, such a gaze is not only phallic and penetrating. It can also be womblike and containing. In "Eros and Psyche" the taboo against any kind of gaze is an excellent example of two partners who are allowed only a limited expression of intimacy. Moreover, the limitation corresponds to their sexual identities and concretizes the male and female roles—Eros as the phallic, penetrating male and Psyche as the receptive female. Psyche's gesture with lamp and knife intentionally shattered both the marriage and the concrete, rigid gender roles it upheld.

The Boldness of Psyche's Knife

We have used the precision of the knife to distinguish male penis from masculine phallus, explore gender assumptions, and examine the phallic aspects of Eros in the tale of "Eros and Psyche." Now let us consider Psyche's knife as a phallic object. We begin at the moment in the story when Psyche's sisters first propose the plan for exposing the identity of Eros. Having heard two conflicting stories about Psyche's husband, they quickly discover that Psyche has never seen Eros and is completely in the dark about his true identity. Their real fear is that he is a god, which would be an intolerable blow to their own status. Having seen the wealth and splendor of Psyche's new home, her sisters now consider themselves to be "nothing better than maidservants to foreign husbands, banished from home and even from [their] native land, living like exiles" (Walsh 1994, 84). They are consumed by envy, just as Aphrodite was consumed by envy of

Psyche at the beginning of the tale. And like Aphrodite, they plot revenge.

The sisters feign concern for Psyche, telling her that she may indeed be married to a monster as the oracle at Delphi had predicted. Never once do they mention their real suspicion, that Psyche's husband is a god. Psyche is inspired, inflamed, and agitated by her sisters' advice. Nevertheless, she boldly appropriates their ideas as her own, makes a plan, and acts on it. Already we can see the presence of the archetypal phallus in the sudden surge of Psyche's energy directed toward another. "She uncovered the lamp, seized the razor, and showed a boldness that belied her sex" (Walsh 1994, 92). Her phallic boldness is not easily blunted, even when she sees clearly that her husband is the beautiful god of love. Her blood is up, so to speak, and it is the knife itself who turns its edge away from Eros.

Psyche's active potency the moment she seizes lamp and knife is in sharp contrast to her behavior up to this point in the story. She submitted to her fate as the fresh incarnation of Aphrodite and to the way in which it separated her from kin and community. She was submissive in marriage, accepting without question or protest the home her invisible husband provided and the terms of the relationship that he defined. Finally, Psyche submitted to her sisters' demand for the truth once she realized that her crude attempt at subterfuge had failed. "I merely attend at night to the words of a husband to whom I submit with no knowledge of what he is like," she tells them (Walsh 1994, 90). Her willingness to adopt her sisters' plan as her own and carry out the deed is the first instance in which we see Psyche not being meekly submissive.

We can use the classical Jungian ideas of anima and animus to designate what is other (strange, different, "not I") and alluring. When we do this, the pertinent question becomes, At this point in Psyche's relationship with Eros, what is other and alluring? Another way to ask this is, How does the animus, as the contra-psychological opposite to a feminine psyche, manifest itself? Each of these questions is an attempt to discover what is different from Psyche's ordinary behavior and complementary to it, resting on the premise that the more ways Psyche has to express herself authentically, the more whole she is. The answers to these questions are essentially the same. Since Psyche is all submission and compliance, the alluring other way of being is decision and assertion. Psyche's animus would manifest in an image that clearly embodies these qualities. The fact that Psyche intentionally breaks the taboo against seeing Eros and is prepared to slay him suggests just how far she is willing to go. She may be following her sisters' advice, but she is asserting her own individual will openly for the first time. The potent phallic knife is an image of the fresh surge of aggressive vitality that she needs to confront Eros.

Psyche still feels the potent surge of phallic energy as she gazes at her husband for the first time. The depth of her hunger to see him, to possess him with her eyes, is completely apparent in the text. It lingers over every gorgeous detail of his body, from "luxuriant hair steeped in ambrosia" to "his dewy wings gleamed white with flashing brilliance" (Walsh 1994, 92–93). Finally, Psyche's phallic gaze discovers the quiver of arrows by which we know the god Eros. She is curious about this weapon, perhaps spellbound by this source of power. Envy does not drive her. In this moment, Psyche is clearly feeling the rush of her own phallic energy, which makes the arrows of Eros inviting as tangible objects that embody her own internal sense of potency. They offer the allure of recognition. The discovery of the arrows inflames Psyche further, intensifying the surge of vitality she feels. In her urge to explore and penetrate, a pure instance of the presence of the archetypal phallus, she is penetrated by the arrow's love potion. Thus we have a neat reversal. The passive Psyche grows bold. She who is penetrated becomes penetrating. In this moment, that character is female, illustrating the idea that the archetypal phallus can become activated in individuals of either sex. More interesting is what this reversal suggests: to penetrate deeply is to be penetrated deeply.

The Keenness of Psyche's Knife

Psyche's bold action does not sever the neck of the devouring monster—according to the sisters' plan—but it does sever the lovers, destroying their original relationship. In a metaphorical sense, Psyche does kill something monstrous—a so-called marriage characterized by a limited and stultifying expression of intimacy. Eros and Psyche's apparently perfect marriage was too much for Psyche's sisters; hence their envy. It was not enough for Psyche, whose original impulse to invite her sisters into her perfect world shows how perfection, too, can be a prison. As Christine Downing observes, "The sisters are not the seductively beautiful anima figures a man might long for as psychopomp . . . but they are Psyche's sisters, precisely the sisters able to push her in the way her soul requires" (1988, 47). Neumann comes to the same conclusion: the sisters embody "a true resistance of the feminine nature against Psyche's situation and attitude, the beginning of a higher feminine consciousness" (1956, 75).

Psyche's sisters express the crude and domineering phallic power that is so often mistaken for phallic potency. Had either one of them wielded the knife someone would have died because they are consciously cruel and clearly envy Psyche's seemingly perfect marriage. As their subsequent behavior proves, they would gladly take Psyche's place. In classical Jungian terms, the sisters are animus possessed, a style of power that has a very distinctive feel to it.

Years ago I worked for a woman whose leadership style made me edgy. I didn't immediately have a label for it, just some plain and simple feelings that took a while to sort through. The feelings included unease, wariness, and a sense that something else was going on, but I didn't know what. As I was pondering my response to her, an image spontaneously arose of an elbow-length velvet glove, deep red like the color of dried blood. The image was odd and oddly persistent. Every time I walked into this woman's office for a meeting, the image came along. Then one day the picture completed itself in a flash: I started thinking of her as "the Velvet Glove" because I knew there was a cold steel fist underneath. This woman played at being warm, concerned, related —quite a bit like Psyche's sisters, in fact—yet this was simply a performance, completely at odds with her deeper motivations which the façade could not quite disguise. Ultimately, the façade was too thin and brittle to disguise her tyrannical aims, as it is with Psyche's sisters.

On the other hand, I know many women who have thoroughly integrated the kinds of power we might associate with the inner masculine; they are not animus possessed. It is as though their phallic power lives at the core of their body, like a strong and supple spine that helps them stand up for themselves, speak with authority, and flexibly adopt different modes of being in a genuinely relational manner. They consistently demonstrate awareness, sensitivity, and compassion no matter how difficult the situation and render judgment, when it is necessary, in a thoughtful and whole-minded way.

Psyche is naïve in many ways, and she is especially vulnerable to her sisters' machinations. She is caught between her loyalty to her sisters, who speak partial truths, and her genuine love for Eros, who speaks partial lies. In Psyche's situation, who wouldn't be confused? As the tale unfolds, it becomes clear that Psyche's self compels her through this morass toward an individual relationship to a beloved and toward her own creative eros. So while Psyche is bold, she is not ruthless or remorseless. Her desire to see and know Eros remained paramount, even at the pitch of conflict when blind acting out would have been understandable. Her actions are archetypally phallic—active, flowing, surging—but that is not all they are. Although her gaze is penetrating when she finally does see Eros, it is important to remember that focus is not only masculine thrust; it is also feminine containment. Psyche could easily have killed her husband, or made a valiant attempt to do so, but she beholds him as the beloved instead.

In the delicate balance of these two inclinations, the phallic urge to penetrate and the uterine (or wombed) urge to contain, Psyche's knife played a key role. It refused to kill either of the lovers. We can read this as an emotional response, a reflective act, or a combination of the two. In any case, the knife's response is characterized by feeling—but so is the lamp's. Whereas the lamp embodies exuberant delight, Psyche's knife embodies restraint. This is very odd behavior for a phallic weapon. Could it be that Psyche's phallic knife teaches us something important about the archetypal phallus? When the dramatic turn of events leaves Psyche physically shaking from a conflicting mix of emotions—aggression and hesitation, erotic arousal and religious awe, fear and love—any one of which could have dominated the situation, Psyche's phallic knife retreats. Could it be that the phallus, which we typically think of as showy and extraverted, also expresses itself through introversion?

This moment in the story alerts us to the idea that Psyche's keen knife can serve love and the soul in many ways. What appears to be impotency is, in fact, a very potent choice. The knife's retreat preserves both Eros and the erotic connection between the lovers. The art of wielding a sharp weapon includes knowing when to keep the blade sheathed. Choosing not to fight when you are perfectly prepared to do so is not weakness, it is wisdom. Restraint is power.

With this in mind, recall that Psyche's knife is in actuality a dagger, a single blade with two sharp edges. Thus it is an image that embodies dualism and an archetype that manifests itself through opposites. We are not meant to understand Psyche's knife only as a masculine, phallic symbol. Psyche's double-edged knife is an image with a double ancestry: it evokes both shining Eros with his erect phallus and the Minoan serpent goddess with her double-headed ax. As an archetypally masculine image, the knife symbolizes Psyche's bold desire to penetrate and connect with Eros. As an archetypally feminine image, the knife symbolizes Psyche's ability to hold Eros in her gaze at the moment she breaks the taboo and in her heart after he leaves. Psyche's actions, which bespeak both her desire and her faith, eventually inspire Eros to create a new and sacred marriage with the soul.

6

YOUR KNIFE

If we don't first disturb the mind's familiar concepts of power,
we can hardly be smart when using it.

—JAMES HILLMAN, KINDS OF POWER

The opposition between love and power is an illusion that begins with our ignorance of power. It has been enshrined in another equally illusory opposition between the feminine and the
masculine. And it lives at the heart of depth psychology, which
frankly ought to know better. For instance, Barbara Sullivan, in
her book *Psychotherapy Grounded in the Feminine Principle*, says,
"Depth psychology also needs to turn radically toward the Feminine, away from power, activity, and success, towards love and
acceptance of life as it really is rather than as we wish it were"
(1989, 109). The idea that to turn toward the feminine is to turn
away from power is irritating, but it reflects a belief I have heard
expressed in many different venues. In casual as well as scholarly conversation, I frequently hear female, feminine, and love
lumped together about as often as I hear male, masculine, and
power treated the same way.[63] The result is that issues of feminine
power go underground—that is, they exist unconsciously—and
find expression in furtive and destructive ways that aren't part of
an integrated set of values. Moreover, it reinforces the idea that
males and the masculine have and use power and that females
and the feminine are powerless. Will we ever develop a more differentiated awareness?

It is far better to ask ourselves, How do I express my power
with those I love? than to believe that power and love are worlds

apart. *What* someone loves reveals their values. *How* they love reveals their character.

Patriarchy, which historically has exhibited an obsession with control, has been justly vilified on this account. Patriarchal systems exercise power through domination, regardless of whether love is allegedly present or not. As James Hillman points out, domination dominates our idea of power, our very thoughts about power, because it is built into the etymology of the word itself. The Latin root of "power" is *potere,* from which we get "potency" and "potential," but also *poti,* which means "husband, lord, or master." Thus Hillman's excellent question: "How can we exercise power, do anything at all as agents, without dominating? It is the great question of our historical psyche, perhaps of human nature: how to act without dominion, without oppressive control, and yet accomplish" (1995, 97–98). Indeed, is it even possible?

Hillman's perplexing question has been taken up by many thinkers. Among my favorites is Ursula Le Guin, who said in a commencement speech to a group of women, "I hope you live without the need to dominate, and without the need to be dominated. I hope you are never victims, but I hope you have no power over other people" (1989, 117). Le Guin's hope is heartfelt but naïve. Most of us will have power over other people at some point, even if it's a slight power or for a fleeting moment. But must it be domination? Her next words give us an answer, in part:

> And when you fail, and are defeated, and in pain, and
> in the dark, then I hope you will remember that dark-
> ness is your country, where your future is. Our roots are
> in the dark; the earth is our country. Why did we look
> up for blessing—instead of around, and down? What
> hope we have lies there. Not in the sky full of orbiting
> spy-eyes and weaponry, but in the earth we have looked
> down upon. Not from above, but from below. Not in the
> light that blinds, but in the dark that nourishes, where
> human beings grow human souls. (ibid.)

I believe Le Guin's words carry a double meaning. The earth nourishes us when we are defeated and wounded, and it is also where we shall discover the power that nourishes us and those we love.

In her memoir *Dance of the Dissident Daughter*, Sue Monk Kidd also uses the metaphor of earth to speak about power:

> In the beginning we wake to find ourselves like trans-
> planted saplings trying to subsist in an unnatural,
> unfriendly (patriarchal) ground. We discover ourselves
> becoming sapless inside, going dry in the place where
> feminine soul rises, animates, and nourishes our lives.
> We know that in order to save our lives as women, we
> have to find new ground. So we set off in search of the
> feminine ground inside the circle of trees. We put down
> roots. And if we are patient, if we are true to ourselves,
> if we are willing to see ourselves through the growing
> seasons, an inevitable thing happens. We become hearty
> women who have our own ground and our own stand-
> ing, sturdy as oak after the winds. We become women
> who let loose our strength, whose truth, creativity, and
> vision fly like spores into the world. (1996, 198)

This persistent metaphor of becoming rooted in the earth up-ends power-as-domination, literally. In growing down we do grow hearty, full of heart, so that we are not easily broken by the fiercest winds. In growing down we develop a rooted stance in the world, inimitable and undeniable. This power is organically whole and so complete in itself that domination is simply beside the point.

Anne Baring also alludes to the earth and to the heart in a fresh definition of the archetypal feminine:

> It is the principle of relationship, the great web of life
> that connects us to each other and to the life around us.
> It stands for the values of the heart and the recognition
> that life on this planet is sacred and that the planet itself
> and all the variety of species it embraces is something to
> be cherished and protected by us rather than exploited
> for the benefit of our species alone. (2009, n.p.)

As we saw in chapter 5, connection also falls within the domain of a male god, Eros, and the masculine phallus signifies the surging desire to connect. But the feminine is behind this larger, felt sense of the connectedness and sacredness of life, and we can follow the Greek tradition of imagining earth, nature, Gaia as feminine. How can we embrace or protect her if we have no power?

In thinking about this question, a Tarot card I had drawn during a recent meditation came to mind: the Princess of Disks. I reflected on my love for "Eros and Psyche" and the end of their story: a marriage blessed by all the gods and Psyche pregnant with Eros's child. In the Tarot deck I use, the Princess of Disks, which is the suit associated with earth, is a beautiful pregnant young woman, like Psyche. She is also a warrior princess, reminiscent of the courageous Psyche I have come to revere. The Princess of Disks holds a shield in her left hand while in her right hand she grips a crystal-headed quarter staff that points down toward the earth. As if to underscore the direction our gaze is meant to follow, she fixes her attention on the earth. "There," she seems to say, "you will find illumination. Go in search of feminine ground."

The Princess of Disks is a very tender image. To those who advocate a more loving and tender approach to life, it may seem to mean turning away from power, activity, and success, the relentless and exhausting striving of our contemporary world. But a closer look informs us of what we can learn from the armed princess: when we love, we accept obligations, and we gain influence. This is power. We may be uncomfortable with that idea, but it doesn't make it any less true.

The tale of "Eros and Psyche" shows us just how much power we have within the context of love. For Psyche, one simple choice, one small move, meant nothing would ever be the same. Moreover, her choice moved the gods, something she could not have foreseen. Psyche's bold act, which shattered an unsatisfying and rigid relationship, alerts us to the actual fluidity of roles and the dynamic balance of power necessary for authentic intimacy. Healthy marriages need this, but so do individual people when they are engaged in the arduous work of becoming themselves.

Becoming ourselves requires time and space within our love relationships and apart from them: the solitude of Artemis side by side with the intimacy of Aphrodite. In many conversations with women who feel the pull toward a larger life, and particularly with those for whom making art is part of that journey, the hunger for an Artemisian refuge is acute, as necessary as food. Something demands that we move outward from a domesticated desire to a wild desire, fiercely lived, in which entire worlds are awaiting our attention. This may partly explain the enduring appeal of Virginia Woolf's *A Room of One's Own*, written eighty years ago, and more recently, *Women Who Run with the Wolves*, the best-selling book by Clarissa Pinkola Estés. My own fascination with armed women certainly is an example of the enduring appeal of wildness. I'm not the only woman who is thrilled by the power of J. R. R. Tolkein's Éowyn, the warrior princess Xena, Buffy the Vampire Slayer, the elegantly ferocious Neytiri, Katniss Everdeen, and their like. I know that such power depends on an embodied sense of ourselves and a deep, sensuous, and reciprocal relationship with the earth. Simply, without genuine ground there is no genuine power.

Why are we particularly fascinated by women's wildness? Take Virginia Woolf as an example. Although she lived and wrote at a time when women had even less control over their own destiny than they do today, she hits on an enduring truth. As part of their gendered upbringing, women are trained to give endlessly to everyone else before claiming time, space, and resources for themselves. It may be that this is a biological imperative, but it is certainly reinforced by cultural expectations. It should come as no surprise that a woman's response to the idea of a room of one's own is often a palpable sense of longing, excitement, and eagerness. Conversely, when she realizes how little of her own space and time she has, we should not be shocked if she feels sorrow, anger, envy, or frustration.

Hence women's turn to the dark earth, because if few human relationships offer women the nurturing womb every creative urge requires—including the urge to create themselves—then they can go to ground, their own ground. That ground can take many forms. For me, it is often the blank page in the darkness just before dawn, when everyone else in the house is still sleeping. For others, it might be a patch of grass in a nearby park, a brilliant expanse of glacial ice at ten thousand feet, or the feel of wet clay as it takes shape on a spinning potter's wheel. In the classic story "A Tree Grows in Brooklyn," the heroine finds her ground on the narrow steel fire escape of her tenement building, shaded by a particular kind of tree that grows tall and lush despite the harsh environment. However or wherever a woman finds it, their ground teaches them feminine power.

Women feel their way into feminine power by developing an embodied sense of vitality and potency. But it takes time, such a long time, in fact, that this kind of power is often associated with the archetypal crone. As Marion Woodman and Elinor Dickson put it so beautifully, "She holds an unspeakable wisdom in the very cells of her body. The beauty and horror of life are held together in love" (1997, 11). Although age does not guarantee one will accrue this wisdom, suffering the slings and arrows of outrageous fortune does have something to do with it.

As we, men and women, respond to what life brings, the crone very gradually presents herself. She can shock us when we hear what comes out of her mouth. She speaks the blunt truth and lets the chips fall where they may. Not that she is without feeling, certainly not without sensitivity. But she has seen enough to be able to separate the irrelevant from the essence, and she has neither the time nor the energy to waste on superficialities (ibid., 10).

You can tell when someone has embodied the crone. It is revealed in a quality of movement and a quantity of stillness, in stature and gesture. Once acquired, it cannot be taken away, only given away.

In "Eros and Psyche," Eros may have provided his beloved with a perfect life that answered all her physical needs when he installed her in his palace, but this was not her ground. Had she remained there, I imagine that she would have slowly become as insubstantial and ghostly as the invisible servants who attended her. I wonder if Psyche's need to see her so-called marriage more clearly was in fact an urge to find her own ground and put down roots in the dark earth. If so, then I like to think that the divine Psyche at the end of the tale becomes a goddess who is earthy, here and now, immanent in creation like her powerful mother-in-law Aphrodite, a blessing on those of us who welcome her.

But as the tale warns us, welcoming her is not without risk. Psyche's struggle alerts us to the painful ordeal we will likely face in the work of creating ourselves. Although you may think of Psyche's knife as a fanciful prop from an old myth, it is not. All of us can, and do, make agonizing choices about those we love that irrevocably change our future and theirs.

If your blade is very sharp, it will cut things together, not apart.

In each of the six chapters of this book, we have explored a facet of Psyche's knife as though we were walking around the image and seeing it from many different sides while asking, How does a sharp blade belong in a story about love and the soul? Here you are invited to apply these ideas to your own life, first to reflect and then to act.

Action is imperative for two reasons. As Jung realized, archetypal images impose on us ethical obligations. They don't just spontaneously arise from the deep layers of the psyche and self-organize into a meaningful pattern at a particular time and place without making a claim on us.[64] Thoughtful, purposive actions honor that claim. Second, action creates experience, and experience is the most potent teacher because it brings an idea down to earth, into the body, where genuine learning happens. Actions, enactment, or what one of my teachers calls archetypal activism, honors our human capacity to respond and transform—to always know ourselves as unfinished and incomplete, in relationship with the living process that we call psyche.[65]

∾

ON BEHALF OF LOST KNIFE

ON COMMITMENTS

"Marriage stands alone in the human imagination as one of the great primary commitments of an individual life," says David Whyte, "but it is also a metaphor for all the other commitments we must make"(2009, 23). This metaphoric approach is a great starting point for thinking about the many ways in which you're married—or, to put it another way, how many marriages you're in.

- *Who and what are you committed to?*
- *What do you give in each marriage and what do you get?*
- *How does your commitment to one marriage support or enhance another?*

- *What do you do when your commitment to one marriage conflicts with your commitment to another?*
- *When do you feel like you are living up to your commitment and when do you feel you are not?*
- *Which marriage consistently takes priority?*

Write a letter to each of your partners—you won't send it, it's for your own reflection—giving yourself permission to speak from the heart about what this marriage means to you. It may seem a little odd to address an inanimate object such as your garden, your unfinished novel, or your high-tech gadget or to write to your horse or your dog, but love letters have been written to the objects of our devotion for centuries. Begin the letter with "Dear garden," or "Dear novel," or "Dear iPad" and imagine that it can hear you. When you finish, read it aloud. You may be surprised by what you discover.

In a journal, describe each commitment and then write your "marriage" vows. You may never have thought of writing vows to your profession or to your art or to yourself at the time you entered into the commitment, but that doesn't mean you haven't made them. Now's the time to discover what they are, as honestly as you can.

If you are married to a person, go back and read the vows you made on your wedding day.
- *What do you think about them now?*
- *What would you add or change to better reflect your experience?*
- *What have you privately vowed, without telling your partner or even admitted to yourself?*

ON CONFLICT

Each of us first learns about conflict among loved ones by watching our parents, siblings, and members of our extended family. Eventually, we may notice how neighbors fight, how a schoolyard bully acts, and what happens to the timid. Because the earliest lessons can become unconscious assumptions, identify and explore your assumptions about conflict with someone you love.

Describe the conflicts you observed between your parents.

- *Did they fight openly or not at all?*
- *Did they raise their voices, throw things, retreat into another room, or walk out the door?*
- *If someone left, how long were they gone?*
- *Who did what to resolve the conflict, or was it ever resolved?*
- *If there was no open conflict, what happened instead?*

Using your reflections in the previous exercise, write a "code of conduct" for how to fight with someone you love reflecting what you actually witnessed, not what you believe is right, fair, or just (the two may be different).

Recall an important conflict you've had with someone you love: boyfriend or girlfriend, partner or spouse.

- *How was your style of fighting similar to what you witnessed in your family?*
- *How does it compare to the code of conduct you just wrote?*
- *What would you like to do differently next time?*

Popular culture also feeds our imagination of conflict and fighting. Spend some time reading novels, graphic novels, playing video games, or watching films to observe how the characters fight.

- *Which hero is your favorite?*
- *Which skills or abilities, especially the ones the hero uses just before, during, and in the aftermath of a conflict, do you admire?*
- *If you could have any of these skills, which would it be and how would you use it?*

If you are familiar with astrology, look up the placement of Mars in your natal chart. Mars, the archetype of war, can suggest something about what rouses your martial energy and the way you fight.

- *What house and sign is Mars in?*
- *Which planets aspect your Mars?*

Consult a professional astrologer or a good book on astrology, such as Laurence Hillman's *Planets in Play* (2007), to find out more.

ON BEHALF OF ALCHEMICAL KNIFE

Literature and myth offer numerous examples of how intimate our enemies are. An implacable enemy can devote more time, energy, and attention to us and our affairs than even the dearest friend. It's a truism that a person can be judged by their enemies. The question is: what can you learn from them?

Think of a personal enemy, someone you know well (or once did), toward whom you feel animosity, even hatred. This doesn't have to be someone you hate all of the time. In fact, this person might even be a friend or lover who has arouses your ire on occasion. Reflect on how this person arouses your anger or hatred and try to name the core issue.

- *How do you express your anger, overtly or covertly?*
- *If you withhold your anger, why?*
- *What would you gain and lose if you expressed your anger openly?*

Jung's notion of the shadow suggests that we make our enemies out of the rejected and despised parts of our own character. A close examination of an enemy can be self-examination if we have the moral courage to look. Consider a personal enemy and write down all of the ways in which you are different from this person. You might try making a list with the same phrase beginning each statement, such as "I don't have this person's _____" or "I don't think/do/say _____ like this person does."

Next, reflecting on that same enemy, create a new list. This time, slowly, thoughtfully, and thoroughly examine all of the ways you are similar to this person. Once again, make a list that begins with a phrase such as "I have this person's _____" or "I think/act/speak like this person when I _____."

Create a mask of your face using clay, wire, papier-mâché, plaster bandages, or some other material that will hold its form. Decorate the outer surface of the mask with images that represent who you are to the world, your public face. Decorate the inner surface of the mask with images suggesting what you hide or keep private, even those things you barely acknowledge to yourself.

Compare the lists you created describing your enemy/yourself to the mask. If you can imagine the two lists and the outer and inner surfaces of the mask in dialogue with one another, what would they say?

ON LUXURIOUS PRISONS

When Eros falls in love with Psyche and whisks her from the cliff to the grounds outside the golden palace, she awakens and walks right into it. There, her every need is taken care of, or so it first appears. On the one hand, this dwelling is a palace, yet on the other hand, it is a kind of prison. This part of the story dramatizes how palaces are also prisons. Since we're speaking metaphorically, a palace, home, or dwelling does not have to be a physical structure that provides for basic needs such as food and shelter. It can also be a situation that structures your life and supplies emotional or spiritual needs such as love, self-esteem, or purpose.

Reflect on the places or situations in your past that have provided for your every need or most of them, one that felt luxurious.

- *What comforts did it offer you?*
- *Which of your needs did it meet?*
- *How did it make you feel safe?*

If you have never had such a place, construct one in your imagination: what would it look and feel like, what would it offer you?

Imagine that place or situation as a fortress with thick walls and a sturdy gate.

- *Who helped you build the walls?*
- *Who and what helps you maintain them?*
- *How long ago did you build them?*
- *What lives outside the walls?*

Create a sketch, drawing, or collage of this place, clearly indicating the strong walls that separate the interior space from the exterior space. Using words or images, put things inside the walls that this place offers you. Do the same for the things that the walls keep out or away. (You could also create this using clay or building blocks or as a sand tray exercise.) Sit back and look at your creation.

- *Is there any element that surprises you?*

- *Do you notice any patterns or themes?*
- *Does something appear both inside the place and outside of it?*

Choose something from within the walls and imagine that it is animated, with feelings of its own or something to say. Engage in a dialogue with it. Next, choose something outside the walls and do the same thing: imagine it as an autonomous figure with its own feelings and engage in dialogue. What do you learn from these animated figures?[66]

ON BEHALF OF SACRIFICIAL KNIFE

ON FIERCENESS

We have seen that fierce females from many different cultures are well armed. Such armaments symbolize skills or abilities and each has their own meaning. For instance, when and where you would use a dagger is different from when and where you would use a thunderbolt. Armaments tell us what a person is prepared to do, when necessary. You decide for whom and why.

Create a drawing of yourself with multiple arms, like the Hindu goddess Durga. Give yourself the armaments you either have or would like to have.
- *What does each one symbolize for you?*
- *What kind of power does it give you?*
- *When would you use it?*

Collect objects that represent these powers and keep them in a meaningful place, arranging and rearranging them as circumstances dictate. For instance, if you're preparing for an important and potentially difficult conversation, you might place the objects that will help you front and center.

Think about the strong women you admire, either from life or in fiction and make a list of them. Take time to reflect on the kinds of power they have and how they express it. Try to describe their individual powers as precisely as possible. For help thinking about power, see James Hillman's wonderful book *Kinds of Power* (1995).

Review your list of strong women and their powers. Identify the powers that you recognize as your own.

- *How and when do you express each one in your life?*
- *What kind of response did it create?*
- *Which powers in the list seem foreign or alien to you?*
- *Which ones make you uncomfortable?*

Popular culture is a mirror in which we can see fantasies of power. In fact, it's more like a hall of mirrors which reflect the changes in those fantasies over time. Do a little pop culture exploration to find out how the qualities of strength, boldness, or fierceness are currently expressed in female characters. For instance, you might start with the current list of best-selling novels or films and video games currently attracting a mass audience and analyze the heroines they depict. What do these incarnations of the fierce feminine say about our culture at this moment in history?

ON DEATH

Feminine consciousness, symbolized by the Great Goddess, suggests a unique understanding of death as part of one continuous cycle of life, death, and rebirth. We die many times over the course of a well-lived life. Such deaths are often portrayed in mythology as a journey to the underworld, a humbling process that ruthlessly strips you of your most cherished ideas and beliefs and produces a new attitude of humility. It is only in retrospect that you can look at the journey as necessary and meaningful.

Think about a death that had a big impact on you, not necessarily the literal death of a loved one, but an ending of something you valued: a home you had to leave, a breakup or divorce, a job you lost.

- *What "died" when this happened?*
- *What did you try to cling to or keep alive?*
- *How has your life changed since then?*

Find a garden that you can visit throughout the year and choose a plant or tree to observe, particularly as the barrenness of winter gives way to spring. If you live in a temperate climate, choose something that changes seasonally, such as a rose bush, since roses are severely pruned in the winter. Notice your feelings about each stage of the plant's life. For instance, when do you feel sorrow or despair and when do you feel joy? Can you feel both at the same time?

One of the major arcana in the Tarot is Death, usually one of the scarier cards that might turn up in a reading. However, skilled interpreters of the Tarot emphasize the symbolic nature of death and how it serves life. Then a productive question becomes, What needs to die? or What do I need to let go of? Compare the Death card from several different Tarot decks. What symbols are prominent and what do they mean to you? Read different interpretations of the card and reflect on them from the perspective of feminine consciousness. Then, using whatever art supplies you prefer, design your own Death card.

ON BEHALF OF LUNAR KNIFE

ON THE WISDOM OF THE BODY

The lunar goddess Artemis can teach us that taming our feelings cuts us off from an important source of knowledge because our emotions are knowledge. They have their own intelligence and can give us insight into complex situations. After centuries of dismissing the body as irrelevant and emotions as dangerous, some of us continue to be resistant more than receptive to what the body knows. Perhaps it is time to honor what Marion Woodman and Elinor Dickson describe as the "unspeakable wisdom in the very cells of the body" (1997, 11).

Think about the last time you had a strong gut feeling about a person or situation.
- *What did you do with this feeling?*
- *Did you dismiss it or pay attention?*
- *Did it become the dominant response or did you factor it in with other kinds of knowledge?*
- *Did you look to others for support or corroboration?*
- *In the end, how much of your gut feeling turned out to be right?*

Find some time and a place where you can safely relax by yourself for a little while. Lie down on your back, close your eyes, and place your hands over your lower belly. Begin to pay attention to your breath and gradually allow it to slow down into a comfortable rhythm.

- *What emotion comes up?*
- *Is it a familiar emotion or one that you push away or repress?*

Make a list of emotions that you feel fairly often, the emotions that are familiar to you. One by one, try to locate the emotions in your body by connecting each one to a place. You might think of this as an anchor point for the emotion. As you reflect on this list, ask yourself how often that part of your body is painful or, conversely, feels completely numb.

Draw a simple picture of your body on a large piece of paper, using one color to create the silhouette. Then, using an assortment of pens or pencils and the information from your list of emotions, add color to the painful areas of your body. Do the same thing for the numb areas, using a different color. Compare the list of emotions and the drawing. What patterns do you notice?

Working with someone you trust, have your partner gently place their hands on a part of your body that wants attention. Breathe into that area for several minutes. What emotions arise? Allow the emotion to intensify to a tolerable level for you, and then invite an image to come forward. Watch the image and, if you are inclined, engage in a dialogue with the image. If you are familiar with Jung's early work in active imagination, you will recognize this simple process.

ON SOLITUDE

If you want to add Psyche's knife to your toolkit or armory, you need to be able to tolerate solitude, perhaps even welcome it. Welcoming solitude is easier for some than for others. Jung, for example, said solitude was "a fount of healing which makes my life worth living" (letter to Gustav Schmaltz, 30 May 1957, quoted in Segaller and Berger 1989, 189). Regardless of whether you are more temperamentally inclined to be social or solitary, the intense process of personal transformation or an intense relationship to your creative work requires at least some solitude. During that time, you won't be available to those you love. To negotiate this, think through the assumptions, beliefs, and fantasies you have about the role of solitude within love relationships.

Reflect on a specific moment with a loved one in which you began to feel separate or alone.

- *How did that moment begin?*
- *Did you withdraw from the other or did it feel more like being abandoned?*
- *What triggered the movement into solitude?*
- *What were your thoughts and feelings about the other person or the situation while you felt solitary?*

Reflect on the solitariness of other couples that has made an impression on you, your parents, for example, or your siblings and their husbands or wives.

- *How often are they apart from each other?*
- *Do they seem content when solitary or, conversely, lonely and unhappy?*
- *How do they move between the two states, being alone and being together?*
- *Did you ever have the feeling that they are alone and unhappy while they are together?*
- *What assumptions about solitude within intimacy do you think they've taught you?*

Take a close look at the art you have hanging on your walls. Pay particular attention to any images that depict solitude and intimacy you've collected over the years and describe the mood and feeling. Do you notice any patterns or themes? Try to stand back and see the collection as a stranger might. What would that person learn about you?

Imagine having a room of your own or, if you already have one, bring that room to mind.

- *How is it furnished and decorated?*
- *What precious possessions do you keep there?*
- *What kinds of music do you listen to, if any?*
- *When do you go there?*

- *How does the room enhance your life?*
- *Who would you happily share this room with?*
- *Who would you keep out and why?*

Create or remodel the room of your own, the actual space if you have it or on paper as an art project if you don't. Feed your imagination of the room by looking through magazines and collecting images of all the things that make this room truly yours and then build a collage to represent it. Play with every sensuous aspect of the room, including colors and textures, light and sound, décor and furniture.

Imagine being with your partner or spouse and wanting to go to the room of your own.
- *What do you need to say or do to make this move?*
- *How much effort does it require?*
- *What kinds of feelings does it arouse?*
- *Once you've entered this room and have your solitude, what kinds of thoughts or feelings about being available to others linger?*

ON BEHALF OF PHALLIC KNIFE

ON POTENCY

We have seen that potency is an inner mental, psychological, spiritual, or physical capacity or strength. Desire and potency distinguish one person from another and, as we age, different potencies play a larger role in our life. You can connect to your potency by becoming aware of your phallic power, since the phallus, as we've seen, symbolizes an inner vitality and flow directed toward what you most desire. You also can detect a future potential, perhaps a capacity or strength you admire in others but have not yet fully developed yourself, through feelings of excitement or challenge, both of which are symbolized by the eager phallus.

Think of people you know now who are potent.
- *How and when do they use their strength?*
- *What particular strengths do they have and use?*
- *What do they create for themselves and others with that strength?*
- *What impresses you most about them?*
- *How would you want to emulate that person?*

Choose a form of potency that most interests you, such as mental strength, spiritual strength, or physical strength, and read biographies of people who exemplify that strength.

- *How did their potency develop over time?*
- *What circumstances shaped it?*
- *How does their potency reflect their personal values?*
- *To what have they dedicated their lives?*

Close your eyes and imagine that your spine is a column of potent energy allowing you to stand up for yourself and others. Describe its color, texture, temperature, and movement. Hold this image for a few minutes and notice the changes in your body.

- *What happens to your breathing?*
- *Where do you feel tension accumulate or dissolve?*
- *If you were to choose a piece of music that celebrates this potency, what would it be?*

While listening to that music, imagine how, when, and where you would use your potency.

In some cultures, children adopt or are claimed by a power animal or totem who accompanies them through life.

- *If you could choose a power animal for yourself, what would it be and why?*
- *What powers would it give you?*
- *In what situations would it make you feel more potent?*

ON RESTRAINT

Genuine power is frequently characterized by restraint because the most capable people rarely need to display their power in an overt, thoughtless, or stupid way. In the Kurasawa film *Sanjuro*, this idea is stated bluntly—the best swords are kept sheathed—a lesson that the brash hero learns from a wise elder woman. To put it differently, if you've got it, you don't need to flaunt it. This may be why Athena, the Greek goddess who is born fully grown from her father's head dressed in battle armor, is also known for the quality of restraint: her flashing eyes are "the emblem of a lucid intelligence that can see beyond the immediate satisfaction" (Baring & Cashford 1991, 339). If you are restrained, you have the power to not use your power until the right moment, which is a useful capacity if you want to make Psyche's knife your own.

Go to a local martial arts studio and ask to observe a class. Notice the posture and gestures of the black belts. Then watch how the junior students (usually wearing white, yellow, or green belts) carry themselves. What differences do you see?

Watch nature documentaries about animals in the wild and note the way the most dangerous predators move as they are stalking their prey and when they are keeping a vigilant eye on their kin.

- *When are they still or restrained?*
- *How do they express their boldness or aggression in such moments?*
- *Which one of these animals would you want to embody the next time you need to be restrained, and why?*

The ability to be restrained requires the use of other powers including careful observation, patience, and imagining all consequences of your actions to the best of your ability. Recall a conflict with someone you love and what led to it.

- *How were you patient and observant?*
- *At what point did restraint give way to action?*
- *What did you lose and gain by being restrained?*

Scan the history of superheroes in popular culture and notice how many of them go in disguise, using their powers only when they have to. Choosing one of your favorites, list the hero's qualities when he or she is in disguise and when she or he is being heroic.

- *How similar are the lists?*
- *How is this superhero consistent, whether disguised or not?*

For each quality that appears on both lists, reflect on how they are expressed covertly and overtly.

- *When is the superhero restrained and what kind of authority or power does this give him or her?*

1. Hamlet makes this comment to Horatio in act 5, scene 2, line 10, shortly after they witness the paltry funeral of Ophelia and acknowledge that even the noblest people become, in the end, common earth.

2. Plato describes the daimon in "Tale of Er," a story of Greek origin in the *Republic*. For a fascinating exploration of this tale and more, see Hillman (1996). I borrow the phrase "shock of incarnation" from another great psychologist, the English Romantic poet and artist William Blake.

3. For the full text, see Apuleius (Walsh 1994).

4. The text appears in the second-century Roman picaresque novel, *The Golden Ass*, written by Lucius Apuleius, although it likely reaches back at least another five hundred years in oral storytelling traditions.

5. Some readers familiar with the philosopher Friedrich Nietzsche will recognize the phrase "will to power," which he developed in his 1886 book *Beyond Good and Evil: Prelude to a Philosophy of the Future*. It is sometimes crudely understood as domination or the dominating impulse in individuals, groups, and cultures. However, the contemporary Nietzsche scholar Robert Solomon explains that it is more accurately translated as "personal strength."

6. I owe James Hillman a debt of immense gratitude for his book *Kinds of Power* (1995) which helped me see through our monolithic ideas about power to the subtle differences between and among particular expressions of power. I believe it is one of his lesser-known books, though to my way of thinking it should be required reading for any of us who care about the subject.

7. Though originally published in 1998 and then again in 2000, *The 48 Laws of Power* has continued to sell well in a variety of formats, including audio and Kindle editions, in the first decade of this century and has been reviewed mostly favorably by nearly 700 readers on the Amazon website. It is a fascinating read, not only for the stories that Greene tells but for the insight he offers into his own world. I found the last part of his dedication particularly poignant: "Finally, to those people in my life who have so skillfully used the game of power to manipulate, torture, and cause me pain over the years, I bear you no grudge and I thank you for supplying me with inspiration."

8. For example, Robert Johnson, one Jungian scholar who published his in-depth study of "Eros and Psyche" in *She: Understanding Feminine Psychology*, speaks about the knife in simple, gendered, and derogatory terms. The knife, according to Johnson, is a symbol for "that devastating capacity

a woman has of impaling a man with a flow of words. . . . This is also one of the ways a man's anima, his feminine side, behaves when he is in poor relation to it. It is cutting and sarcastic; it comes with knife in hand" (1976, 25). He goes on to describe "our law" which is "to use the lamp and *not the knife*" (p. 25, emphasis added). I'm not quite sure who Johnson means to include in the pronoun "our," but his "law" is highly suspect and not particularly psychological. This may be why the discussion of the sisters and the knife is considerably different in the revised 1989 edition of this book. Though Johnson still credits Psyche's sisters with more responsibility than I do—"Psyche quickly falls under the spell of this [sisterly] advice" (22)—his view of this portion of the story is more balanced. For instance, Johnson says, "The questioning sisters are a frightening spectacle, for, though they are the harbingers of consciousness, there is the danger that you can be caught in their stage of development and remain destructive for the rest of your life. Just as you can stay on the mountain of Death and see men as purveyors of disaster, so you can also be caught in the stage of the two sisters and destroy anything that a man tries to create" (1989, 24).

Other authors whose work is thoughtful, thorough, and penetrating omit mention of the knife entirely. Two that particularly surprise me are Nor Hall and Marion Woodman. For instance, in Hall's *The Moon and the Virgin*, she says: "In the old story, Psyche, the maiden, was urged by her bitterly jealous sisters to light an oil lamp at night to look upon the body of her lover, who she had never seen. What she had known in the dark was lovely to her, but her sisters planted a gnawing seed of doubt when they suggested that it was not a youthful god in her bridal bed but a horrible, monstrous snake. A fatal drop from her curious, sputtering lamp sent Eros, the beautiful boy god, soaring heavenward out of sight and embrace of the girl. In a flash she had seen and lost and then began her exhaustive, nearly endless search for reunion" (1980, 20). A few pages later Hall repeats the omission of the knife by saying: "Psyche in that original stunned moment [is] caught holding the lamp by which she betrayed her lover" (p. 22).

Similarly, Marion Woodman and Elinor Dickson, who summarize the tale of Eros and Psyche in *Dancing in the Flames*, speak about the lamp and forget the knife: "Then Psyche's shadow sisters, jealous of her good fortune, tell her she is sleeping with a monster, perhaps a serpent that does not want his secret discovered. With that seed of doubt planted in her mind, she eventually lights her lamp while her husband is asleep, goes up to him and sees the divine Eros" (1997, 129).

9. Many authors, including Marie-Louise von Franz (1980, 89) and Erich Neumann (1956, 78), interpret the sisters as the man-hating voices of the matriarchy, an aggressive consciousness that thinks of all marriage as a monstrous incursion into the feminine world. In *Psyche's Sisters: Reimagining the Meaning of Sisterhood* Christine Downing points out that the tale was written intentionally to foster this impression (1988, 49). From one perspective, the sisters' behavior seems to be a textbook example of unintegrated animus. They "hand" Psyche a masculine phallic weapon

to act out their own malicious envy. But in the hand of the archetypally feminine soul, who is both deeply and individually connected to Eros, this phallic weapon and the confrontation it assists become something entirely different.

10. Ironically, this couplet (1.3.218–219) appears at the end of Brabantio's speech just after he hears that his daughter Desdemona had fallen in love with the "the Black Othello" and married him of her own free will. For Brabantio, this is a reprehensible act of disobedience that has clearly wounded his vanity.

11. Schwartz-Salant's book *The Mystery of Human Relationship* is a profound exploration of the alchemy of transformation. He reminds us that "an alchemical approach . . . is not primarily concerned with what people do to one another, such as through projections onto one another, but instead with their experience of a field both people occupy" (1998, 7). In the case of Psyche and Eros, this field is fully populated by a human girl, her divine lover, and a lamp and knife with their own distinctive ethical positions, which I will explore in the next chapter.

12. For further discussion particularly from a Jungian point of view, see Baring and Cashford (1991), Douglas (1989), Johnson (1976, both editions), Neumann (1953), Perera (1981), Rowland (2002), Sullivan (1989), Ulanov (1971), Ulanov and Ulanov, (1994), von Franz (1970), Woodman (1980, 1985, 1987, 1993), and Woodman and Dickson (1997). For Jung's point of view, see his chapter on anima and animus in "The Relations between the Ego and the Unconscious" (1928).

13. The extended discussion of the anima and soul in Hillman's *Anima* (1985) is excellent, as is Thomas Moore's popular book *Care of the Soul* (1992). I also highly recommend Sylvia Perera's *Descent to the Goddess* (1981).

14. Becoming a real fragment, according to Edinger, requires the ability to give birth metaphorically. The gestation period may be long and arduous, with others threatening the life of the "child" within. Such danger, however, can intensify the mother's protectiveness. Sometimes, the pregnancy is invisible even to the mother for a long time: we have not yet found the way in which we are unique, and many years go by before we discover it. Regardless of how and when the birth takes place, it is only by becoming a real fragment that we can relate to the eternal whole. In his autobiography *Memories, Dreams, Reflections*, Jung says it this way: "In knowing ourselves to be unique in our personal combination—that is, ultimately limited—we possess also the capacity for becoming conscious of the infinite. But only then!" (1961, 325). Psyche has this knowledge and this capacity. She sacrifices the unreality of the original relationship with Eros to play a real part in her own story.

15. According to Hillman (1975), psychologizing is one of the four natural activities of the soul.

16. Rendering the image in one of these media is a crucial stage in what Jung, in the 1935 Tavistock lectures, came to call "active imagination."

He first described the technique in his 1916 essay "The Transcendent Function" and, over the years, refined his idea and his name for it. It was the cornerstone of his own creative illness, as he describes in *Memories, Dreams, Reflections* (1961, 192–193), and it assumed crucial importance in his life's work. For instance, in his essay "On the Nature of the Psyche" (1954b), in his "Commentary on 'The Secret of the Golden Flower'" (1957), and in *Psychological Types* (1921), Jung would say that active imagination is a more effective way of working with the autonomous images of the psyche than dream interpretation because it involves the cooperation of consciousness with unconscious contents. In the Tavistock lectures he makes this quite plain: "Often in a later stage of analysis, the objectification of images replaces dreams. The images anticipate the dreams, and so the dream-material begins to peter out. The unconscious becomes deflated in so far as the conscious mind relates to it. Then you get all the material in a creative form and this has great advantages over dream-material. It quickens the process of maturation" (1935, par. 399).

17. Medieval alchemists, inspired by the fantasy of turning lead into gold, developed an elaborate language to observe and understand the transformation of matter. Jung adopted alchemy as an extended metaphor to describe the transformational processes of the psyche. This language was particularly helpful in approaching the unconscious as a *complexio oppositorum* because it embraced paradox and resisted simplification. Alchemy did not try to resolve the opposites contained within a unity, but let them stand.

18. This is true regardless of gender, a point Neumann misses in his emphasis on "the approach of the male" and its consequences for the bride (1956, 63).

19. Thomas Moore offers a lovely insight: "I feel as a married person that every day I die to my single life, to a certain kind of freedom, and to my historical self, not in a bad way, but definitely a death" (personal communication, December 2011).

20. "Consuming envy is a major barrier individuals confront in their search for a more individuated self," says Labouvie-Vief, which certainly describes Psyche's sisters (1994, 166).

21. This grounding gives Eros the time he needs to begin healing from the inside out, to choose whether to remain immobile and inflexible in his anger toward Psyche or eventually to soften. In the end, Eros is unable to resist the allure of his beloved. Neither Psyche nor Eros demonstrates an ability to respond thoughtfully and with individual discernment to their antagonistic situation. Each is wounded and blind: there is something that they do not or cannot see, weigh, and act upon. The complex sequence of events and assumptions that nearly leads to murder and suicide, and which does lead eventually to the sisters' deaths, demonstrates the inherent dangers of the monocular vision that plagues Psyche, her sisters, and Eros. But since this is Psyche's story, the emphasis falls on her naïveté.

22. The focus on beauty in Psyche's last task is a theme that C. S. Lewis poignantly explores in his novel *'Til We Have Faces* (1956). One of Psyche's sisters, Orual, narrates this modern retelling of the myth. She is notably ugly and, as she grows into maturity and becomes an accomplished ruler and a skilled swordswoman, Orual learns to veil her ugliness. As a result, she becomes as mysterious, remote, and sphinxlike as the Great Goddess her clan worships. This goddess, the story's Aphrodite, is a great lump of dark stone housed in an ancient stinking temple. Lewis draws a clear parallel between the ugly, powerful sister who shows no understanding of the independent movement of Psyche's eros and the ugly, cold, and immovable stone. At the end of this tale, the ointment Psyche retrieves for the stone Aphrodite is really intended for the stony and implacable Orual. But beauty cannot be applied like a cosmetic. It is innate, not an adornment, and Psyche's sister realizes this too late. Lewis clearly uses physical beauty as a metaphor for the inner beauty, warmth, and tenderness of archetypal eros. Perhaps this is an unconscious homage to a pagan deity: Aphrodite—quite apart from her son Eros—is the goddess of love, beauty, and desire, though we only see her spiteful aspects in "Eros and Psyche." Psyche, who retains her tender and loving nature throughout the story, carries the beautiful aspect of Aphrodite. She continues to be a fresh incarnation of the goddess of love, which is how the story begins. But Psyche never does see this about herself, not even at the very end of the tale when every trial she has endured expresses the compelling beauty of her soul.

23. Four also symbolizes the parts, qualities, and aspects of the One, which in Jungian terms symbolizes the Self who orchestrates our individuation (for further reading, see Jung 1948, par. 176, and 1937, par. 140).

24. As described by von Franz (1992) in her work on "The Golden Ass." Psyche's story also demonstrates the value of patient, careful work, very like the work of the alchemist. In fact, Psyche shares two very important similarities with an alchemical adept. First, she submits herself to the transformational opus. Over the course of the story, she will demonstrate the perseverance that sustained medieval alchemists through their arduous trials. Second, Psyche is not working alone. Just as a male-female pair conducted alchemical experiments, Psyche's invisible partner, her true partner, is archetypal eros. Its presence is signaled by the appearance of Pan, the great god of cosmic nature who symbolizes the fecund aliveness of the great round. Pan encourages Psyche to pursue Eros and to have faith in love. Thus Pan is the voice of eros who speaks on behalf of archetypal eros, launching Psyche on her fateful journey.

25. The method I am using, amplification, is borrowed from Jung, who discovered that enriching a single image (in this case Psyche's knife) with images from other cultures and other times provides a context that often reveals aspects of the original image that would otherwise go unnoticed. This is a hermeneutic move that honors an archetypally feminine sense that images are related to one another and can be best understood through

pondering their relationships. I described the methodology in greater detail in my dissertation (2001).

26. Schwartz-Salant's discussion is particularly interesting to me because it is based on his clinical experience of encountering patients who have discovered this original power. He says of such patients, "It is as if she had taken hold of the power she once only knew in an unconscious manner" and "has an ego grasp on its roots . . . from a feminine archetypal source." Then he candidly goes on to describe his experience as a male witness to this power: "It can be quite shocking to be faced with a woman entering this domain, her natural birthright. From compliance and the readiness to please, albeit with a good deal of guiding helpfulness that many may have wonderfully appreciated, a woman gains an authority that can go against and beyond anything that I as a man can know" (1982, p. 111). I have sensed this power in myself and seen it in others. In one unforgettable instance, I felt the power uncoil inside my body like animal awakening. The energy traveled up my spine over the curve of my skull and pooled in my eyes so palpably that my vision changed. But I doubt I would have remembered this particular moment had it not been for my teacher's reaction: she shuddered and asked, "What was *that?*" I didn't know, not then.

27. Baring and Cashford (1991, 131) argue that Minoan culture appears to be entirely centered on a feminine god image. No archaeological evidence of a male god exists.

28. Baring and Cashford (1991, 113) conjecture that the priestesses of the serpent goddess held these axes during ritual ceremonies to honor her.

29. For millennia, wherever our Paleolithic ancestors recorded their stories in painted images on cave walls and sculpted objects of exquisite beauty, snakes have been associated with females, both human and divine—despite the fact that the snake is also considered a phallic symbol. For modern readers unfamiliar with the ancient artifacts, the associations between serpents and women is probably most clear through the Judeo-Christian stories linking Eve with the serpent in the Garden of Eden. But in that patriarchal tradition, both serpent and woman became the embodiment of evil.

30. Baring and Cashford (1991, 114) comment that though the ax of the Minoan goddess is clearly similar to axes carried by men and male god-images, it shouldn't be interpreted as a weapon. Gimbutas (1977, 281) asserts that "weapons are nonexistent in Old European imagery, whereas the dagger and battle-axe are dominant symbols of the Kurgans, who like all historically known Indo-Europeans, glorified the lethal power of the sharp blade." See also Gimbutas 1982.

31. Since much of this art is schematic, Gimbutas points out that "scholars can recognize little more than insect head or insect hands. Whether she is 'Lady Bee' or 'Lady Butterfly' cannot be determined" (1982, 185).

32. Gimbutas (1989, 186) notes that at this time butterfly images are engraved on double-headed axes.

33. Gimbutas argues that the symbolic meaning of ax and butterfly is further reinforced by two other images that group themselves around goddess figures: the bird claws of the vulture and owl goddesses, who presided over death and rebirth, and the vulva, which symbolizes the origin of life or regeneration (1989, xv, 245). All of these images—ax, butterfly, vulture, owl, vulva—suggest transformation.

34. According to Gimbutas (1989, 161), doubling suggests intensification and progressive duplication, "hence potency or abundance." The development of the embryo in a mother's body, in a process called cell mitosis, is a good example of progressive duplication. This fits nicely with Jung's discussion about the meaning of the numbers one and two. Whereas one symbolizes potential, the world of spirit, and possibility, two symbolizes matter coming into form or creativity. With two, Jung says, "multiplicity and reality begin" (1955–56, par. 659).

35. Let's pause a moment and actually practice complexity. Can we definitively say that doubling is the exclusive attribute of the goddess? Shouldn't we look closer, seeking subtle intimacies between superficially incompatible ideas and images? When we do, doubling appears to belong to both the archetypal masculine *and* the archetypal feminine. On the one hand it includes the male god Eros, who symbolizes the urge toward connection—think of thousands of sperm swimming toward the egg so that cell mitosis can begin. On the other, it includes the female goddess who symbolizes progressive duplication of cellular life—cell mitosis and the cellular differentiation that ultimately produces new life. The irony should be obvious: what could be more appropriate than that the most basic pair of opposites we can imagine, male and female, would jointly rule the archetypal idea of the pair?

36. Phallic power is one form of power, not the only form of power. There are specifically feminine forms of power that many experts have not recognized as readily, perhaps because they are not quite as obvious as the phallus, which is a bit of an exhibitionist (see chapter 5).

37. For a full and beautiful discussion of the symbolism of the naked sword and the love potion, see John Haule's *Pilgrimage of the Heart* (1992).

38. Spielrein is wrongly credited with anticipating Freud's death instinct, which he outlined in *Beyond the Pleasure Principle* approximately nine years later. Her thesis was, in fact, the exact opposite of Freud's. He believed that sexuality was the only life instinct and that the end purpose of all other instincts is a return to our original inorganic condition. Or, as Freud pithily stated it, "The aim of all life is death" (quoted in Gay 1989, 615). Freud conjectured that the sexual instincts "are the true life instincts. They operate against the other instincts, which leads, by reason of their function, to death; and this fact indicates that there is an opposition between them and the other instincts" (ibid.).

39. The second part of Henry IV, act 3, scene 2, line 235, from *The Riverside Shakespeare*, edited by G. Evans (1974, 906).

40. Elsewhere I have written of "Eros and Psyche" as a tale of psycho-

logical vampirism, using the vampire archetype to explore the monstrosity of their original relationship in the palace of Eros (see Nelson 2009).

41. "According to the ancient view," Jung notes, "the moon stands on the border-line between the eternal, aethereal things and the ephemeral phenomena of the earthly, sublunary realm" (1955–56, par. 173). Thus the lunar knife tells us that Psyche crosses into a liminal state between the earthly and the divine.

42. For the full story, see West (1988).

43. This is reflected in Freud's advocacy of ego control. "Our best hope for the future," Freud says, "is that intellect—the scientific spirit, reason—may in process of time establish a dictatorship in the mental life of man. The nature of reason is a guarantee that afterwards it will not fail to give man's emotional impulses and what is determined by them the position they deserve" (1933, 212). To be fair to Freud, he published this at a time when Europe had recently emerged from one devastating war and a fanatic in Germany was intentionally cooking up a xenophobic frenzy that would result in the deaths of fifty million people in less than a decade, including two thirds of Europe's entire Jewish population. He had good reason to fear that cool reason would be drowned in a hot tide of emotion. Marie-Louise von Franz once accounted for the difference between Jung and Freud in archetypal terms: "They served different gods," she said. "Jung's way was matriarchal, open to the irrational and imaginal, he believed in letting the unconscious live and even submitting to it" (quoted in Hall 1980, xv). There is a place in Jung's cosmos for the psychic tides of life and the feminine moon that rules them.

44. On this topic, David Abram comments that the sensuous body is "a kind of open circuit that completes itself only in things, and in the world. . . . I am a being destined for relationship: it is primarily through my engagement with what is not me that I effect the integration of my senses, and thereby experience my own unity and coherence" (1996, 130, 125).

45. We have examined Psyche's allies as an epiphany of two female deities, Gaia and Artemis, but her allies adopt male forms, too. For instance, Pan the goat god is the first deity to guide Psyche on her journey. Zeus's bird, the eagle, helps her complete the third task. The tower, which we can view as a masculine phallic symbol, prevents Psyche's final attempt at suicide and advises her on the journey to the underworld. Finally, her male lover Eros awakens Psyche from the Stygian sleep at the end of the fourth task and guides her to Olympus.

When we look closer, there is a provocative connection between the green of Nature and the fertilizing male seed (Jung 1955–56, par. 137). Fecundity, from an archetypal perspective, can be masculine or feminine. To make this point, let's consider a passage from Jung's late work *Mysterium Coniunctionis* where he discusses blessed greenness. Though Jung is describing the loneliness of the Shulamite, he could just as easily be describing the lonely travails of Psyche, and so the feminine pronoun has been substituted for the masculine.

The state of imperfect transformation, merely hoped for and waited for, does not seem to be one of torment only, but of positive, if hidden, happiness. It is the state of someone who, in her wanderings among the mazes of her psychic transformation, comes upon a secret happiness which reconciles her to her apparent loneliness. In communing with herself she finds not deadly boredom and melancholy but an inner partner; more than that, a relationship that seems like the happiness of a secret love, or like a hidden springtime, when the green seed sprouts from the barren earth, holding out the promise of future harvests. It is the alchemical *benedicta veriditas*, the blessed greenness, signifying ... the secret immanence of the divine spirit of life in all things. (Jung 1955–56, par. 623)

The blessed greenness in this passage expands our understanding of Psyche's inner partner in the work. She is Artemis, the archetypal midwife of the soul. He is Eros, the soul's beloved. We need not insist that this inner partner be one gender or the other. As the Self, this partner is an archetype of wholeness—neither female nor male or both female and male.

We can also view the hidden partner Jung mentions above from an alchemical perspective. Just as the *soror mystica* assisted an alchemical adept with the opus—the two symbolizing the male-female pair that united in the *coniunctio*—the god Eros is continually present to Psyche. Of course in Apuleius's myth, there is an obvious and interesting reversal. Psyche is the adept, a role traditionally assumed by a male, while Eros plays the part of the mystical sister. Yet he is clearly a masculine and phallic figure in the myth. Psyche's journey is toward the masculine Eros; he is her guide. The erotic, in its fullest sense, shapes and contains her journey; it is the medium. As we'll see in the next part, Eros as an active, quick archetype of desire shares the volatile and connecting quality of the medium in alchemical work, the *spiritus Mercurius*. Once again, Psyche's knife will shine forth as an alchemical blade that cuts things together, not apart.

46. Jung's interpretation of the child is quite different from Freud's, where the child seems to draw us back into our personal history to a very early age where the bedrock of character was laid down and could be changed very little, if at all.

47. Jung speaks elsewhere (1952a, p. 37) about completeness as a feminine ideal.

48. Aldo Carotenuto speaks movingly about the "underside of love" that must emerge for a whole relationship (1987, 10).

49. In *Anatomy of the Psyche* (1985), Edinger speaks about the development of substantial individuality using the metaphor of the alchemical process of *coagulatio*, which occurs in two distinct phases in an individual life. The first *coagulatio* phase strengthens the personality sufficiently to tolerate an encounter with the Self. The second phase of *coagulatio*, which is the actual engagement with the Self, further consolidates the personal-

ity. This stage, Edinger says, is identical with the individuation process because continual encounters with the Self guide the individual toward wholeness.

50. As Jung suggests, this is a far more difficult problem. Yet this "reconciliation between apparently incompatible opposites" is the very essence of the *coniunctio* (1955–56, par. 790). Furthermore, it is the goal and supreme realization of the work of alchemy and of individuation. The opposites that need to be reconciled in the work are "either confronting one another in enmity or attracting one another in love" (ibid., par. 1). Aphrodite and Artemis are neither lovers nor enemies—except distantly, on the occasion of the Trojan War, when they stood on opposite sides of the conflict. Neither are they particularly fond of one another. In general, they avoid each other entirely. What sort of *coniunctio* do they represent in the myth of "Eros and Psyche"?

51. This may well describe Psyche's desire, although if so, it is not fully conscious. We don't have an insight into Eros's feelings since he remains sequestered for most of the rest of the story. We can infer from his actions that his love also deepens and matures. Eros risks his mother's impressive wrath and rescues Psyche when she fails to complete the fourth task. He then petitions Zeus to sanctify their union. More convincing is the transformation we see between the last moment he spends with Psyche before abandoning her and his return at the end of the myth. When both his shoulder and his pride are burned, Eros's farewell speech is truly hateful. His hatred softens as his shoulder heals.

52. Downing says that "in Artemis' realm, feelings do not issue in creative expression or in sexual involvement. One does not do anything with them; one simply comes to know them, discriminatingly, unflinchingly" (1981, 172).

53. Hillman defines archetypes as "constitutional propensities . . . instinctual patterns of behavior . . . [and] ordering structures of the psyche" that are part of our common inheritance (1975, 35). Whitmont describes them as the "foundation stones of the psychic structure, which in its totality exceeds the limits of consciousness and therefore can never become the object of direct cognition" (1991, 198).

54. Although masculine and feminine are useful explanatory tools, they can too easily become oppressive weapons in the wars between the sexes. Popular culture fosters the heavy-handed, thuggish approach to psychosocial distinctions. Turn on the television, for instance, and you'll see our most petty, unthinking behavior on display night after night. In fact, it is extremely difficult to use words like *masculine* and *feminine* thoughtfully. Among the many authors who strive for thoughtfulness, Nor Hall says it well: "I am taking care to say 'the feminine' here rather than 'female' or 'womanly' to stress its roving home. Femininity is a mode of being human that can be lived out (and betrayed or suppressed) by both men and women" (1980, 4).

55. See, for instance, the critique by Andrew Samuels of anima theory in which he says that analytical psychology assumes "that there is something eternal about femininity and, hence, about women; that women therefore display certain essential transcultural and ahistorical characteristics; and that these can be described in psychological terms. What is omitted is the ongoing role of the prevailing culture in the construction of the 'feminine' and a confusion develops between what is claimed to be eternal and what is currently observed. . . . It is here that the deadweight of archetypal theory is felt" (1985, 98).

56. Jung rarely offers a balanced portrait of the animus but speaks at length and dogmatically about its negative manifestation. For example, Jung says that we can detect the presence of the negative animus in a woman's "inferior judgments, or better, opinions," her "inferior logos," her "inaccessible prejudice," and in her "opinion which, irritatingly enough, has nothing to do with the essential nature of the object" (1957, par. 60). See also Jung's *Symbols of Transformation* (1952b, par. 462), and "The Relations between the Ego and the Unconscious" (1928, par. 335). This has led Andrew Samuels to comment that "there is little doubt that Jung saw the anima as a more pleasant figure than the animus. In his books anima seems to soften and render a man more full of soul, whereas animus, on the other hand, he more often portrayed as leading a woman into aggressive ex cathedra pronouncements, mania for facts, literalness, and so on" (1985, 214).

57. Esther Harding (1965) describes the shadow archetype as "not I" but with two important differences between the shadow and the anima/animus. First, the shadow is often uncomfortably familiar, that is, there is a vague sense of recognition, and second, the individual's emotional response, especially in the first few shadow encounters, is usually shame or repugnance, not attraction

58. Comparing prominent women in the public eye can also help us see how gender is culturally produced to serve political ends. One might be curious to know about the private life of a First Lady and how she exerts her power within the marriage, and outside the marriage, when not exposed to the glare of media attention. I suspect that more gender fluidity is possible for both partners within the private sphere and that social, cultural, and political pressures tend to enforce traditional expressions of gender and power in the public sphere.

59. Despite this larger reading of Freud and the penis, it is still clear that Freud was limited by his own physiology in understanding the phallus. As evidence, we can ponder his odd phrase "phallic mother," which is an attempt to describe the enormous power and potency of mother especially vis-à-vis the child. As a nineteenth-century male, Freud's only recourse for envisioning female power was to append a male penis onto a female body. Even if we don't read this image literally, the conclusion is telling. For a woman to be powerful, she must borrow or put on attributes of the male. Ironically, this move was more archetypal than Freud realized

in the sense that a woman, regardless of whether or not she is a mother, can have a phallus.

60. Other authors have adopted this approach also. Thomas Moore, for instance, equates a larger-than-life erection to the vitality of eros as a creative principle (1998, 39 ff).

61. I appreciate this reframing of phallic power by Lacan and others for a personal reason. Several years ago I consciously chose not to be a mother. In order to decide against having children, I first had to understand pregnancy and birth as metaphors for creativity. In other words, I needed to reflect on and redefine my relationship to the creative principle. The deciding question for me, many years ago, was not, Will I give birth to my own children? but What will I give birth to? In lengthy and sometimes excruciating conversations with my closest girlfriends, some of whom were mothers already and some of whom longed to be, we arrived at an archetypal understanding of our literal wombs that was a profound awakening for each of us. To this day, my girlfriends and I still talk about that experience. I can only imagine (and hope) that a similar journey for a man, from penis to phallus, might result in an equally profound restructuring of his relationship to his own erotic vitality and deep creativity.

62. The classic study of this difference is Carol Gilligan's *In a Different Voice* (1993). It called into question our models of healthy development by pointing out that our standards have derived from male experience and represent male values of the solitary hero who proves himself by going it alone.

63. This assumption is reflected in the symbolism just beneath the surface of *Men Are from Mars, Women Are from Venus*, John Gray's best-selling book. It's catchy and true enough: women and men are like two different species, and learning to get along might work better if we start with that premise. My point is that Venus is another name for Aphrodite, the goddess of love, and Mars is another name for Ares, the god of war, so, once again, we see the simplistic equation of women and love versus men and power.

64. Jung develops the idea of ethics and archetype in his long essay "On the Nature of the Psyche" where he says "confrontation with an archetype is an ethical problem of the first magnitude" (1954b, par. 410). But this ethical problem is only understood and faced by people who recognize responsibility for their psychic health, which Jung equates with becoming whole and which "has remarkable effects on ego-consciousness. . . . The ego cannot help discovering that the afflux of unconscious contents has vitalized the personality, enriched it and created a figure that somehow dwarfs the ego in scope and intensity" (par. 430).

65. Stephen Aizenstat (2009) has developed the concept of archetypal activism over thirty years of working with dreams. Doing something on behalf of the dream image, such as making an offering or creating and participating in a ritual, is usually the final step in working with a dream. It is a particularly powerful moment because it honors the aliveness of the dreamer and the dreaming psyche.

Paolo Freire, in *Pedagogy of the Oppressed*, speaks eloquently on behalf of education as a lifelong process in which individuals become more human through reflection and action. He says, "problem-posing education affirms men and women as beings in the process of becoming—as unfinished, uncompleted beings in and with a likewise unfinished reality. Indeed, in contrast to other animals who are unfinished, but not historical, people know themselves to be unfinished; they are aware of their incompletion. In this incompletion and this awareness lie the very roots of education as an exclusively human manifestation. The unfinished character of human beings and the transformational character of reality necessitate that education be an ongoing activity" (1997, p. 65).

66. If you are familiar with Jung's work, you will recognize this as active imagination. For more information, see *Jung on Active Imagination*, edited by Joan Chodorow (1997), or *Inner Work* by Robert Johnson (1986).

Abram, D. 1996. *The Spell of the Sensuous*. New York: Vintage Books.

Aizenstat, S. 2009. *Dream Tending*. New Orleans: Spring Journal.

Auden, W. H. 2007. *Selected Poems*, 2nd ed. Edited by E. Mendelson. New York: Random House.

Baring, A. 2009. "The Dream of the Cosmos: A Quest for the Soul." Retrieved January 2009 from www.annebaring.com/anbar20.

Baring, A., and J. Cashford. 1991. *The Myth of the Goddess: Evolution of an Image*. New York: Arkana/Penguin.

Barz, H. 1991. *For Men, Too*. Translated by K. Ziegler. Wilmette, IL: Chiron Publications.

Becker, E. 1973. *The Denial of Death*. New York: Free Press.

Berry, P. 1982. *Echo's Subtle Body*. Dallas: Spring Publications.

Bettelheim, B. 1982. *Freud and Man's Soul*. New York: Vintage Books.

Bettelheim, B. 1989. *The Uses of Enchantment*. New York: Vintage Books.

Boer, C., trans. 1970. *The Homeric Hymns*. Chicago: Swallow Press.

Campbell, J. 1991. "The Mystery Number of the Goddess." In *In All Her Names*, edited by J. Campbell and C. Muses (pp. 55–129). San Francisco: Harper San Francisco.

Camus, A. 1968. *Lyrical and Critical Essays*. Edited by P. Trody. Translated by E. Kennedy. New York: Alfred A. Knopf.

Carotenuto, A. 1987. *Eros and Pathos*. Translated by C. Nopar. Toronto: Inner City Books, 1989.

Carson, A. 1998. *Eros, the Bittersweet*. Normal, IL: Dalkey Archive Press.

Chodorow, J. 1997. *Jung on Active Imagination*. Princeton, NJ: Princeton University Press.

Cook, E., ed. 1990. *John Keats*. Oxford, England: Oxford University Press.

Corbett, L. 1996. *The Religious Function of the Psyche*. New York: Routledge.

Cousineau, P. 1994. *Soul, an Archeology*. San Francisco: HarperSanFrancisco.

de Beauvoir, S. 1959. *Memoirs of a Dutiful Daughter*. Translated by James Kirkup. New York: World Publishing Company.

Douglas, C. 1989. *The Woman in the Mirror: Analytical Psychology and the Feminine*. Boston: Sigo Press.

Downing, C. 1981. *The Goddess: Mythological Images of the Feminine*. New York: Crossroad, 1992.

Downing, C. 1988. *Psyche's Sisters: Reimagining the Meaning of Sisterhood*. New York: HarperCollins.

Edinger, E. 1985. *Anatomy of the Psyche*. LaSalle, IL: Open Court.

Edinger, E. 1992. *Ego and Archetype*. Boston: Shambhala.

Edinger, E. 1994. *The Mystery of the Coniunctio*. Translated by J. Blackmer. Toronto: Inner City Books.

Eisler, R. 1987. *The Chalice and the Blade*. San Francisco: Harper and Row.

Estés, C. P. 1992. *Women Who Run with the Wolves*. New York: Random House.

Fraser, A. 1988. *The Warrior Queens*. London: Arrow Books.

Freud, S. 1933. *New Introductory Lectures on Psycho-analysis*. Translated by J. Strachey. New York: W. W. Norton, 1965.

Freire, P. 1997. *Pedagogy of the Oppressed*. New York: Continuum.

Gay, P. 1989. *The Freud Reader*. New York: W. W. Norton.

Gilligan, C. 1993. *In a Different Voice*, 6th ed. Cambridge, MA: Harvard University Press.

Gimbutas, M. 1977. "The First Wave of Eurasian Steppe Pastoralists into Copper Age Europe." *Journal of Indo-European Studies* 5:277–289.

Gimbutas, M. 1982. *The Goddesses and Gods of Old Europe, 6500–3500 B.C.* Berkeley: University of California Press.

Gimbutas, M. 1989. *The Language of the Goddess*. New York: HarperCollins.

Gray, J. 1992. *Men Are from Mars, Women Are from Venus*. New York: HarperCollins.

Greene, Robert. 1998. *The 48 Laws of Power*. New York: Penguin Books, 2000.

Gustafson, A. 2011. "Women and the Archetype of the Phallus: Engagement with the Sculpture of Louise Bourgeois." Doctoral diss., Pacifica Graduate Institute.

Hall, N. 1980 *The Moon and the Virgin*. New York: Harper and Row.

Hamilton, E., & H. Cairns, eds. 1961. *The Collected Dialogues of Plato*. Princeton, NJ: Princeton University Press.

Harding, E. 1965. *The I and the Not-I*. Princeton, NJ: Princeton University Press.

Harding, S. 1996. "Gendered Ways of Knowing and the 'Epistemological Crisis' of the West." In *Knowledge, Difference, and Power*, edited by N. Goldberger, J. Tarule, B. Clinchy, and M. Belenky (pp. 431–451). New York: Basic Books.

Haule, J. 1992. *Pilgrimage of the Heart*. Boston: Shambhala.

Hillman, J. 1972. *The Myth of Analysis: Three Essays in Archetypal Psychology*. Evanston, IL: Northwestern University Press.

Hillman, J. 1975. *Revisioning Psychology*. New York: Harper Colophon.

Hillman, J. 1983. *Archetypal Psychology: A Brief Account*. Dallas: Spring Publications.

Hillman, J. 1985. *Anima: An Anatomy of a Personified Notion*. Dallas: Spring Publications.

Hillman, J. 1995. *Kinds of Power: A Guide to Its Intelligent Uses*. New York: Doubleday.

Hillman, J. 1996. *The Soul's Code*. New York: Random House.

Hillman, J. 1997. *Suicide and the Soul*, 2nd edition. Woodstock, CT: Spring Publications.

Hillman, L. 2007. *Planets in Play*. New York: Penguin.

Johns, C. 1989. *Sex or Symbol? Erotic Images of Greece and Rome*. London: British Museum Press.

Johnson, A. G. 2005. *The Gender Knot: Unraveling Our Patriarchal Legacy*. Philadelphia, PA: Temple University Press.

Johnson, B. 1988. *Lady of the Beasts*. San Francisco: Harper and Row.

Johnson, R. 1976. *She: Understanding Feminine Psychology*. New York: Harper and Row. Revised edition: 1989, HarperPerennial.

Johnson, R. 1986. *Inner Work: Using Dreams and Active Imagination for Personal Growth*. New York: HarperCollins.

Jung, C. G. 1916. "The Transcendent Function." In *CW*, vol. 8. Princeton, NJ: Princeton University Press, 1960.

Jung, C. G. 1921. *Psychological Types. CW*, vol. 6. Princeton, NJ: Princeton University Press, 1971.

Jung, C. G. 1928. "The Relations between the Ego and the Unconscious." In *CW*, vol. 7. Princeton, NJ: Princeton University Press, 1953.

Jung, C. G. 1931. "Marriage as a Psychological Relationship." In *CW*, vol. 17. Princeton, NJ: Princeton University Press, 1954.

Jung, C. G. 1933. *Modern Man in Search of a Soul*. Translated by W. Dell and C. Baynes. New York: Harcourt, Brace & World.

Jung, C. G. 1935. *The Tavistock Lectures*. In *CW*, vol. 18. Princeton, NJ: Princeton University Press, 1976.

Jung, C. G. 1937. "Psychology and religion." In *CW*, vol. 11. Princeton, NJ: Princeton University Press, 1958.

Jung, C. G. 1943. "On the psychology of the unconscious." In *CW*, vol. 7. Princeton, NJ: Princeton University Press, 1953.

Jung, C. G. 1948. "A psychological approach to the dogma of the Trinity." In *CW*, vol. 11. Princeton, NJ: Princeton University Press, 1958.

Jung, C. G. 1951. *Aion. CW*, vol. 9ii. Princeton, NJ: Princeton University Press, 1959.

Jung, C. G. 1952a. "Answer to Job." In *CW*, vol. 11. Princeton, NJ: Princeton University Press, 1958.

Jung, C. G. 1952b. *Symbols of Transformation. CW*, vol. 5. Princeton, NJ: Princeton University Press, 1956.

Jung, C. G. 1954a. "The Archetypes of the Collective Unconscious." In *CW*, vol. 9i. Princeton, NJ: Princeton University Press, 1959.

Jung, C. G. 1954b. "On the Nature of the Psyche." In *CW*, vol. 8. Princeton, NJ: Princeton University Press, 1960.

Jung, C. G. 1954c. "Psychological Aspects of the Mother Archetype." In *CW*, vol. 9i. Princeton, NJ: Princeton University Press, 1959.

Jung, C. G. 1955–56. *Mysterium Coniunctionis. CW*, vol. 14. Princeton, NJ: Princeton University Press, 1963.

Jung, C. G. 1957. "Commentary on 'The Secret of the Golden Flower.'" In *CW*, vol. 13. Princeton, NJ: Princeton University Press, 1967.

Jung, C. G. 1961. *Memories, Dreams, Reflections.* New York: Vintage Books, 1989.

Jung, C. G., and C. Kerenyi. 1951. *Introduction to a Science of Mythology.* London: Routledge and Kegan Paul.

Keen, S. 1991. *Fire in the Belly.* New York: Bantam.

Kerr, J. 1993. *A Most Dangerous Method: The Story of Jung, Freud, and Sabina Spielrein.* New York: Vintage Books.

Kidd, S. M. 1996. *Dance of the Dissident Daughter.* New York: HarperOne.

Labouvie-Vief, G. 1994. *Psyche and Eros.* Cambridge, England: Cambridge University Press.

Lacan, J. 2002. "The Signification of the Phallus." In *Ecrits: A Selection,* translated by B. Fink (pp. 271–280). New York: W. W. Norton.

Le Guin, U. K. 1989. *Dancing at the Edge of the World.* New York: Harper-Collins.

Lewis, C. S. 1956. *'Til We Have Faces.* London: Harcourt, Brace and Company.

Mahdi, L., S. Foster, and M. Little, eds. 1987. *Betwixt and Between: Patterns of Masculine and Feminine Initiation.* La Salle, IL: Open Court.

Mogenson, G. 1992. *Greeting the Angels: An Imaginal View of the Mourning Process.* Amityville, NY: Baywood Publishing.

Monick, E. 1987. *Phallos, Sacred Image of the Masculine.* Toronto: Inner City Books.

Moore, T. 1992. *Care of the Soul: A Guide for Cultivating Depth and Sacredness in Everyday Life.* New York: HarperCollins.

Moore, T. 1994a. *Dark Eros: The Imagination of Sadism,* 2nd rev. ed. Woodstock, CT: Spring Publications.

Moore, T. 1994b. *Soul Mates.* New York: HarperCollins.

Moore, T. 1998. *The Soul of Sex.* New York: HarperCollins.

Murray, A. 1935. *Murray's Manual of Mythology.* New York: Tudor Publishing.

Nelson, E. 2001. Psyche's Knife. Unpublished dissertation, Pacifica Graduate Institute, Carpinteria, CA.

Nelson, E. 2009. "Monstrous Desire: Love, Death, and Marriage from Eros and Psyche to Edward and Bella." Proceedings of the 7th Global Monsters and the Monstrous Conference, September 14–17, 2009, Oxford. http://www.inter-disciplinary.net/wp-content/uploads/2009/08/Nelson-paper.pdf.

Neumann, E. 1953. *The Fear of the Feminine.* Translated by B. Matthews, E. Doughty, E. Rolfe, and M. Cullingworth. Princeton, NJ: Bollingen, 1994.

Neumann, E. 1956. *Amor and Psyche: The Psychic Development of the Feminine.* Translated by R. Manheim. Princeton, NJ: Princeton University Press, 1971.

Otto, W. 1954. *The Homeric Gods.* New York: Pantheon Books.

Paris, G. 1986. *Pagan Meditations: The Worlds of Aphrodite, Artemis, and Hestia.* Woodstock, CT: Spring Publications.

Patton, L. 2007. Hinduism. In *Encyclopedia of Sex and Gender: Culture, Society, History*. 4 vols. Edited by Fedwa Malti-Douglas. Detroit: Macmillan Reference USA.

Perera, S. 1981. *Descent to the Goddess*. Toronto: Inner City Books.

Rilke, R. M. 1975. *Rilke on Love and Other Difficulties*. Translated by J. Mood. New York: W. W. Norton.

Rilke, R. M. 1993. *Letters to a Young Poet*. Translated by S. Mitchell. Boston: Shambhala.

Robbins-Dexter, M. 1990. *Whence the Goddess*. New York: Teacher's College Press.

Romanyshyn, R. 1989. *Technology as Symptom and Dream*. New York: Routledge.

Rose, J. 2007. Kali. In *Encyclopedia of Sex and Gender: Culture, Society, History*. 4 vols. Edited by Fedwa Malti-Douglas. Detroit: Macmillan Reference USA.

Rowland, S. 2002. *Jung: A Feminist Revision*. Cambridge, England: Polity Press.

Samuels, A. 1985. *Jung and the Post-Jungians*. London: Routledge.

Samuels, A. 1989. *The Plural Psyche*. London: Routledge.

Schwartz-Salant, N. 1982. *Narcissism and Character Transformation*. Toronto: Inner City Books.

Schwartz-Salant, N. 1998. *The Mystery of Human Relationship*. London: Routledge.

Segaller, S., and M. Berger. 1989. *The Wisdom of the Dream*. Boston: Shambhala.

Shakespeare, W. 1974. *The Riverside Shakespeare*. Edited by G. Evans. Boston: Houghton Mifflin Company.

Shanley, J. 2009 (January). Review of *Doubt. Performances Magazine*, pp. P6 and P7.

Spielrein, S. 1912. "Die Destruktion als Ursache des Werdens" ["Destruction as Cause of Becoming"]. In *Psychoanalysis and Contemporary Thought* 18(1):85–118, translated by S. K. Witt, 1995.

Stein, R. 1998. *The Betrayal of Soul in Psychotherapy*. Woodstock, CT: Spring Journal Books.

Stone, G. 1999. *A Glossary of the Construction, Decoration and Use of Arms and Armour in All Countries and in All Times*. Mineola, NY: Dover Publications.

Storr, A. 1988. *Solitude, a Return to the Self*. New York: The Free Press.

Styron, W. 1990. *Darkness Visible: A Memoir of Madness*. New York: Random House.

Sullivan, B. S. 1989. *Psychotherapy Grounded in the Feminine Principle*. Wilmette, IL: Chiron Publications.

Tarnas, R. 1991. *The Passion of the Western Mind*. New York: Harmony Books.

Taylor, C. 1989. *The Sources of the Self*. Cambridge, MA: Harvard University Press.

Thompson, L. 1999. *Daggers and Bayonets in History*. Staplehurst, Kent: Spellmount, Ltd.

Tolkein, J. R. R. 1955–56. *The Return of the King*. New York: Houghton Mifflin.

Ulanov, A. 1971. *The Feminine in Jungian Psychology and in Christian Theology*. Evanston, IL: Northwestern University Press.

Ulanov, A., and B. Ulanov. 1994. *Transforming Sexuality: The Archetypal World of Anima and Animus*. Boston: Shambhala.

Vandiver, E. 2001. *Classical Mythology* (audio lectures). Chantilly, VA: The Teaching Company.

von Franz, M.-L. 1970. *An Introduction to the Psychology of Fairy Tales*. New York: Spring Publications.

von Franz, M.-L. 1980. *Alchemy*. Toronto: Inner City Books.

von Franz, M.-L. 1992. *The Golden Ass of Apuleius: The Liberation of the Feminine in Man*, rev. ed. Boston: Shambhala.

Walsh, P. G., trans. 1994. *Apuleius: The Golden Ass*. Oxford, England: Oxford University Press.

West, M. L., trans. 1988. *Hesiod: Theogony and Works and Days*. Oxford, England: Oxford University Press.

Whitmont, E. 1982. *Return of the Goddess*. New York: Continuum, 1997.

Whitmont, E. 1991. *The Symbolic Quest*, rev. ed. Princeton, NJ: Princeton University Press.

Whyte, D. 1997. *Fire in the Earth*. Langley, WA: Many Rivers Press.

Whyte, D. 2009. *The Three Marriages*. New York: Riverhead Books.

Williams, J. 1999. *Sex, Portraits of Passion*. New York: The Ivy Press.

Wolkstein, D. 1991. *The First Love Stories*. New York: HarperPerennial.

Woodman, M. 1980. *The Owl Was a Baker's Daughter: Obesity, Anorexia Nervosa, and the Repressed Feminine*. Toronto: Inner City Books.

Woodman, M. 1985. *The Pregnant Virgin*. Toronto: Inner City Books.

Woodman, M. 1987. "From Concrete to Consciousness: The Emergence of the Feminine" in L. Mahdi, S. Foster, and M. Little, eds. *Betwixt and Between: Patterns of Masculine and Feminine Initiation* (pp. 202–222). La Salle, IL: Open Court.

Woodman, M. 1993. *Conscious Femininity*. Toronto: Inner City Books.

Woodman, M., and E. Dickson. 1997. *Dancing in the Flames: The Dark Goddess in the Transformation of Consciousness*. Boston: Shambhala.

Woolf, V. 1929. *A Room of One's Own*. New York: Harcourt, Brace and Company, 1957.

INDEX

Abram, David, 162n44
active imagination, 157n16, 167n66
Aizenstat, Stephen, 166n65
alchemy, 46, 63, 164n50; *coagulatio*,
    163n49; *extractio*, 40, 42–43, 45;
    language of, 23, 158n17; *separatio*, 23,
    40–41, 79, 81, 97; of transformation,
    157n11
allies, 95
amplification, 112, 159n25
Anath, 54
androgyny, 112
anima, 110–11, 129, 156n8, 165n55; and
    soul, 157n13
anima mundi, 46
animus, 110–11, 129, 156n9
animus possession, 131
Aphrodite, 18, 39–40, 42–45, 98, 123–
    24, 159n22; and Artemis, 84–86,
    95–96, 104–7, 164n50
Apuleius, Lucius, 16, 103, 155n4
archetypal: feminine, 59, 60, 71, 73,
    88, 89,111–12, 119; masculine,
    65, 111–12, 119; midwife, 98, 99;
    perspective, Psyche's knife as, 23;
    phallus, 110, 129, 132; psychology,
    62; womb, 124–25
archetypes, 164n53
Artemis, 73, 84–86, 91–99, 148,
    162n45; and Aphrodite, 104–7,
    164n50
Athena, 152
Auden, W. H., 65
Avatar (film), 74, 102
ax: cultic, 56; double, 55–57, 59, 68–69,
    71

Baring, Anne, 53, 136, 160n27, 160n28,
    160n30
Barz, Helmut, 113
beauty, 159n22; internal and external,
    44
Becker, Ernest, 80

Begas, Reinhold, 14
Bellona, 54
Berry, Patricia, 110
Bettelheim, Bruno, 13
Blake, William, 155n2
Bourgeois, Louise, 116
British Museum, 15
butterfly, 57–59

Campbell, Joseph, 53, 63
Canova, 14
Carotenuto, Aldo, 163n48
Carson, Anne, 122
Cashford, Jules, 53, 160n27, 160n28,
    160n30
castration anxiety, 115
catastrophic thinking, 26
child archetype, divine, 101
Collins, Susanne, 74
coniunctio, 75, 94, 105–6
contrasexuality, 111
Corbett, Lionel, 58
crone, archetypal, 92, 139

daggers, 14–16, 31, 68, 108, 133
daimon, 1, 20
Damocles's sword, 59
de Beauvoir, Simone, 79
death, 26, 37–38, 44, 81–82, 97, 117;
    proximity to life, 58–59; and the
    scythe, 86–87; and sexuality, 77;
    symbolic, 78–80, 98
Demeter, 39
depression, 97–98
depth psychology, 110, 134
Dickens, Charles, *Bleak House*, 96
Dickson, Elinor, 8, 139, 148, 156n8
Disney, Walt, 10
divine child, 101
doubling, 60
doubt, 78–79
Downing, Christine, 81–82, 115, 131,
    156n9, 158n19, 164n52

173

Kali, 54, 70–71, 74
Keats, John, 49
Keen, Sam, 113–14, 118
Kidd, Sue Monk, 136
knives, 5–6; alchemical, 23, 36, 46, 47, 50; as symbols, 16; Bronze Age and Early Iron Age, 15; and daggers, 14–16, 31, 68, 108, 133

Labouvie-Vief, 158n20
Lacan, Jacques, 117
language, 16
leave-takings, 50–51
LeGuin, Ursula, 68–69, 135
Lewis, C. S., 159n22
logos, 16
Logos-cutter, 23
loss, 49
love (loving), 93–94, 101, 106; agon of, 102; and conflict, 21 (*see also* relationship, and conflict); and power, 7–10, 134, 137

Machiavelli, Niccolo, 8
marriage, 26–27, 30, 35, 94, 125, 141; sacred, 50; to death, 45, 79
marriage (feminine) container, 125–27
Mars, 69, 166n63
masculine, archetypal, 161n35
masculinity, 111–12, 114, 118, 125
Minoan culture, 55–56
Monick, Eugene, 118
moon weapon, 86, 88
Moore, Thomas, 1, 28, 108, 110, 115, 118, 120, 124, 127, 166n60
Morrigan, 54
myth and mythology, 23, 25, 53, 86–87

Neith, 70, 73–74
Neumann, Erich, 13, 53, 63, 101, 131, 158n18, 158n19
number four, 45
number two, 60

Obama, Michelle, 112
Odysseus and Penelope, 126

Pallas, 54
Pan, 37, 98, 159n24, 162n45
Paris, Ginette, 104
patriarchy, 8, 135

penis, 108–9, 112; autonomy of, 113–14; different from the phallus, 110, 114–15, 128; exhibitionism, 117
penis envy, 115
Perera, Sylvia, 21
Persephone, 44
perspective: developmental, 45; Eros as, 49; multiple, 61; Psyche's knife as, 23, 112; soul as, 75
phallic energy, 116, 121, 130
phallus: archetypal, and arousal, 118; and connection, 118–21; and creative flow, 117–18; desire for, 115; and domination, 119–20; and fertility, 115; sacred, 115
Plato, 1, 122
Pollock, Jackson, 120–21
potency, 135; androgynous, 64–65; feminine, 9–10, 139; masculine, 110, 115, 118; phallic, 131; Psyche's, 129–30
power, 68, 108–9, 134–36, 146–47; and control, 8; corrupted, 8 (*see also* tyranny); as differentiation, 35–36, 42, 47; female (feminine), 54–55, 66, 68–75, 86, 88, 90–92, 116, 139, 160n26, 165n59; and goddesses, 54, 66; and language, 16; and love, 7–9, 141; phallic, 65, 116–17, 120, 124, 131, 151, 161n36; social organization of, 68; uterine, 117
pregnancy and childbirth, 99
prison, 27, 29, 63, 76, 90, 97, 145
privacy, erotic, 124–25
Psyche: as alchemical adept, 159n24; as soul, 3; deification, 45; her failure, 46–47; her four tasks, 18, 36, 39–46, 98, 159n22; inability to discriminate, 29, 35, 44; incarnation of Aphrodite, 25–27; isolated, 25–26, 29; and knives, 30–31; locations in her journey, 50; naïveté, 35, 101, 103, 132, 158n21; ruthlessness, 37–38; vulnerability, 33–34
Psyche's knife, 34–36, 42, 47, 105, 132–33, 140; analogous to the moon, 85; from an archetypal perspective, 23; characteristics, 14; as dagger, 14–16, 31, 68, 70, 71, 74, 108, 133; as dramatis personae, 32; as a fine tool, 36; neglected, 10–11; in paintings or

Lightning Source UK Ltd.
Milton Keynes UK
UKHW021303020122
396478UK00005B/435

9 781888 602531